PRAISE FOR
A Beginner's Guide to Losing Your Mind

"This is a funny, brutal, kind, sobering, remarkably brave, and clear-eyed book. Compelling and necessary."

—Warren Ellis, author of *Normal*, *Gun Machine*, and *Transmetropolitan*

"This book isn't just brilliantly written and welcoming in its tone; it's honest, practical, and important. It is going to help so many people—including friends and family who desperately want to help a loved one but don't know how."

—Emma Gannon, author and podcast host of *Ctrl, Alt, Delete*

"Emily Reynolds is a brilliant writer on an important subject. And hilarious too. I need to go and do another thing now, which is annoying, 'cause I can't stop reading this brilliant, brilliant book."

—Adam Rutherford, author and presenter of Radio 4's "Inside Science"

WHEN YOU'RE NOT F*CKING FINE

WHEN YOU'RE NOT F*CKING FINE

A Beginner's Guide to Anxiety, Depression, and Understanding Your Mental Health

EMILY REYNOLDS

sourcebooks

Published by Sourcebooks
P.O. Box 4410, Naperville, Illinois 60567-4410
(630) 961-3900
sourcebooks.com

Originally published in 2017 in the United Kingdom by Yellow Kite, an imprint of Hodder & Stoughton Limited.

Printed and bound in the United States of America.
POD 10 9 8 7 6 5 4 3 2 1

TABLE OF CONTENTS

INTRODUCTION

Being diagnosed with bipolar disorder was the happiest moment of my life. Forget falling in love, graduation, the birth of my nephew—all that schmaltzy, saccharine stuff pales in comparison to hearing the words "You have bipolar disorder type 1." Meeting the love of your life? Not a big deal, really. Throwing your graduation cap in the air as the symbolic climax of four years of intellectual challenge and growth? Whatever. Sitting in a boxy, gray office as a psychiatrist tells you that, yes, you *do* have a chronic mental illness? Now THAT'S what I'm talking about.

I'm being flippant, but it's really not much of an exaggeration. My road to diagnosis was long and hard, peppered with hours of numb staring in indistinguishable waiting rooms, and it was ten years between the first signs of mental illness and an eventual diagnosis. Ten years of psychiatrists and general practitioners and badly trained counselors, ten years of misdiagnosis and medication that made me sick or fat or even more ill. I can reel off the names of the pills I've taken—SSRIs and MAOIs and tricyclic antidepressants and atypical antipsychotics—like a child drably reciting the periodic table by rote. I've been diagnosed with major depression, borderline personality disorder, bipolar disorder type 1, and a good smattering of "you'll probably feel better in a few weeks." I've accepted, rejected, then finally accepted my status as "someone with mental health problems." It's been a journey in the sense that it has been a grueling physical challenge, and also in the *American Idol* sob story sense. So, while it might just be the beauty of narrative hindsight, the day I was diagnosed felt like a culmination of all of these elements.

I first experienced mental health problems when I was around thirteen or fourteen years old. They seemed to come on unprompted, and at first I couldn't really put my finger on what was wrong or how I was even feeling. Groggy, a lot of the time, with a lack of concentration that I put down to regular disinterest in school and my peers. Then I started to get dizzy—so much so that I felt as if I was floating outside of my own body, unable to cling onto any of my sensory abilities whatsoever. (I later learned that this is what's referred to clinically as *dissociation*—a detachment from physical and emotional surroundings.) I would gaze out of the window on the bus home, looking at houses and shops fly past but not being able to connect the images to anything I could even remotely identify as my "self."

I was also viciously sad; I would sleep almost constantly and had absolutely no interest in anything, and the only thing that would alleviate the stagnant numbness was an addiction to self-harm that I indulged at home and in the school toilets at lunchtime. I didn't think I could possibly be ill, though—I didn't even entertain the idea.

The problem partly lay in the fact that many of the symptoms of depression, or bipolar disorder, are similar to traits that are also considered to be ubiquitous in teenagers. The difference was the severity and duration, but that's hard to communicate when you're fifteen, terminally shy, and haven't got the language to express what you're feeling, full stop. I'd also skimmed the Wikipedia article for Sartre and viewed my malaise as some kind of profound existential statement about the world. It was like the terrible feelings of suffocation were a logical, intellectual choice, a personality trait or a philosophy I'd chosen, rather than an illness that had any power over me.

They weren't. I was depressed.

I was finally diagnosed, ten years later, during the midst of my worst ever depressive episode. I had dealt badly with a breakup, and days spent crying over my ex had turned into weeks of not getting out of bed, and eventually a few months of almost complete stasis. I barely ate, I saw nobody, I did nothing but sleep and cry. I actually cried so much that in the end I became physically unable to muster a solitary tear, and it took nearly a year of stable, medicated living before I was able to cry again. Incidentally, I eventually ended up crying over a dog food ad. It wasn't quite the significant cinematic experience I was hoping for, but y'know, I'll take what I can get.

I knew I was ill when I realized that I was no longer even slightly bothered about my breakup. All the sobbing and sleeping and the inability to eat, not knowing whether today would finally be the day I conjured up enough courage to throw myself under a bus, was actually because I was deeply unwell. It kind of sucked, actually, because at least the breakup had been something to focus on. Where was I without it?

You might think that realizing I was ill, understanding the parameters and cycles of depression, would have made it all a lot easier. I was used to the rigmarole of the routine, after all: feeling shitty for a while, going to the doctor and getting some medication, settling down after some nausea and tooth-grinding, and then feeling okay again. But this time it was somehow harder; something inside me was proving such a profound source of resistance that I was absolutely incapable of doing anything.

I really don't know what did it, but one day that resistance snapped, and I felt that it was imperative for me to go to the doctor as soon as I possibly could. So I did. I went to a clinic to see a doctor I'd never seen before. I was apprehensive, but only as much as anyone normally is when they go to the doctor. But when I told her I was suicidal, she dismissed it immediately.

"Why are you sad?" she asked, having failed to even glance at my extensive medical notes. I explained that there was no reason—I was just ill. But she kept pressing—there MUST be a reason. I kept saying there wasn't, my already pretty weak resolve faltering with every question. Halfway through the consultation, after I told her to actually look at the notes that would corroborate what I was saying, she asked me whether I was interested in giving up smoking.

Eventually she sent me away, telling me that if I was still suicidal "in two weeks" I should come back and see her. It didn't seem to cross her mind that if I was no longer suicidal in two weeks, it would be because I was dead. Even my local mental health trust couldn't help me; I needed to be referred, or sectioned, and I had neither qualification. At the hospital, I *was* handed both a leaflet for Alcoholics Anonymous and a tissue, so I suppose they beat the GP, if only in terms of paper consumption.

I was defeated. Crushed and small and defeated. I was filled with a sick, desperate urgency that clawed at everything I did, and that was seemingly incommunicable. I felt nauseated with despair, and with a restless, unfulfilled desire to do something, although what I wasn't sure. It had been a ceaseless effort to move from bed to bathroom; now, I had somehow dragged myself to the hospital—only to be told I wasn't quite ill enough.

Luckily, I managed to get an appointment to see a great private psychiatrist, who took the time to listen to me and properly evaluate my situation.

I think I already knew I had bipolar disorder—or, at the very least, it was probably quite obvious to anyone who had spent more than five minutes with me when I was manic. One of my friends told me that the first time we ever met, I'd spewed a nonstop, nonsensical torrent of word soup at him for twenty minutes, before announcing I was off to meet up with an ex-boyfriend and left.

I'd also, at various times, got myself deeply into debt, relocated across the country—twice—and signed up and started three degree courses, only one of which I managed to finish.

My life had mainly been defined by my periods of depression, though—the teenage years of Morrissey fandom and self-harm had come at such a persona-defining time that I'd never thought of my mania (by which I mean having grandiose ideas, sometimes delusions, being overactive) as a problem. I think I saw it more as just "the way I am." A more exaggerated version of who I was, maybe, but still a far more accurate and desirable version than the laconic, unwashed slob I became when depressed. I'd never thought of my mania as being problematic purely because it was so much fun—the nights out, the sparkling conversations I thought I was having, the way I felt absolutely, unimpeachably sexually magnetic.

It was only once I moved to London, after I dropped out of university and before my terrible breakup, that I realized how massively mania impacted my life; I was emotionally and physically reckless in a way that alarmed and eventually alienated my close friends. I was bad with money but had no student loan or parental handouts to fall back on. I had a full-time job as well as a packed social schedule that involved endless parties and up to six dates per weekend. I needed less sleep than usual, but it was still profoundly exhausting. I started to conceptualize my mental health differently—maybe it wasn't the dark, motionless days of depression that really defined my state of mind, but the insatiable need for stimulation that came with mania as well.

Throughout my journey from undiagnosed teenager to fully paid-up member of the Certifiably Insane Club, my mental health irrevocably affected almost every area of my life. My education, career, family life, sex life, self-image—every single way in which a person can relate to themselves and the world—were all ruined by my mental health. I've learned the hard way how not to date when you're ill, how to communicate your illness (or not) to colleagues, how best to navigate the rocky road of medication and therapy. I wish I'd had someone to tell me all of this, though, wish I hadn't messed up so many friendships and relationships and jobs with my inability to accept that my bipolar disorder puts obstacles in my path.

So, here is this book. There wasn't a book like this when I was going through all of these things, and I wish there had been, so I've written it. Don't get me wrong. I've read plenty of self-help books, but when you're unable to even *take a shower*, a book that tells you how to *focus your mind on success* or suggests you *ask the universe for the things you want* kind of falls short. All I want to do is ask the universe: "Make me not ill, pal. I just wanna be able to wash my hair like everyone else."

There are books about mental health, too, but they've never really resonated with me or my experiences. There are narcissistic misery memoirs that romanticize the fuck out of mental illness and offer these wild ideas of *redemption through love* or some other nonsense, and there are clinical textbook-type books that offer no emotional insight into illness. There was never anything that bridged the gap between "I identify with this person's experience, and it helps me feel less alone" and "This is genuinely useful advice that I can apply to my own life."

So here we are.

I'd hope that by the end of this book, other people with similar experiences, or maybe totally different ones, will be able to understand their mental health problems a little better, or at least have gathered some ideas on how to effectively manage them. I hope you can avoid some of my horrible mistakes, or at the very least feel comforted that you're not the only one who blurts out your diagnosis on a date, or who lives like a trash-raiding raccoon when you're depressed.

For those who aren't ill, I hope this provides a small insight into what it's like to live with a chronic mental health problem, shatters a few myths, and gives you a rough framework from which you can support the people in your life who might be affected too.

Sometimes this book will be sad, and sometimes it will be brutal—we'll be looking at self-harm, suicide, drug abuse, and more. These chapters might be hard to read, especially if you have experience with the topics. All of the chapter titles are clearly marked, so please do give yourself a break if you think the subject matter might negatively affect you. It'll also be gross, because the reality of mental illness often is, but it might make you laugh as well. There are guides and lists throughout the book, so there's a practical element, too. I'm loath to call it self-help because self-help books can so often be trite and useless, but my hope is that some part of it will make you feel comforted, empowered, or slightly less alone.

CHAPTER 1
DIAGNOSIS

It was an unseasonably brisk October evening when I strode out of my psychiatrist's office with a piece of paper that said I definitely had something wrong with me. For the first time in months, I felt something that vaguely resembled hope, and while I wouldn't go so far as to say I was positive, I felt buoyed by this unexpected life jacket, surprised at how snugly it fit. As he somberly delivered his diagnosis, I had thought to myself, *Don't look too happy, Emily. He'll think you're making it all up.*

I've already said it was the happiest day of my life, and I meant it. Although I was obviously still deeply depressed, all the horrible buzzing noise in my head that told me things would never improve briefly ceased. I felt calm, steady and determined. I felt ready to get better.

Unfortunately, the reason I was so serene was that my understanding of what it meant to "get better" was wildly off the mark.

I saw "knowing what was wrong with me" as the very first step on the journey to sanity, the end of the tangled ball of string that would eventually lead me to the Minotaur that was my mental illness. I thought that being armed with self-knowledge (and a hefty dose of antipsychotics) was some kind of magical key to a previously unknown realm in which breakthrough and profundity were the order of the day.

This is not how it works.

What I had failed to take into consideration was my relationship with myself—my self-image. The way I conceptualized myself as a girlfriend or a daughter—or just as a person—was all tightly bound up with mental illness, correct label be damned. It didn't matter if I was bipolar or depressed or had borderline personality disorder—I might as well have flipped through the *DSM** and randomly jabbed my finger at a set of diagnostic criteria. What really mattered, and what I failed to understand that day, was how much of my personality was dependent on a vague, nebulous concept of "mental illness," rather than on a strict scientific definition.

And, of course, aside from this, a diagnosis can often be completely arbitrary. Studies have shown that, despite standardized

---

* The DSM—or *Diagnostic and Statistical Manual of Mental Disorders*, to give it its full name—is the handbook from which doctors and psychiatrists diagnose particular symptoms and conditions. It's pretty ubiquitous—you won't find a psychiatrist without one—but has also experienced its fair share of controversy with regards to overdiagnosis, validity, and the medicalization of human experience. *Saving Normal* by Allen Frances covers this far better than me!

diagnostic criteria being widely used in the Western world, different doctors can diagnose identical sets of symptoms as totally different conditions. There are cultural differences, too—what are considered to be social norms in some cultures can be pathologized in others. So, it turns out, diagnosis is not the most important element of the mental health journey.

The thing about mental illness—in whatever guise, under whatever name—is that it plagues you with profound self-doubt. "Am I really depressed?" you ask yourself, "or am I just lazy? Is my inability to hold onto money because I have manic episodes, or am I just an irresponsible person? Is my near constant craving for chemical stimulation a coping mechanism I've developed to deal with my problems, or do I just really, really like drugs?"

It's an annoying voice in your ear, like a director's commentary endlessly droning over all the best bits of the film.

Obviously some parts of your life *are* affected by mental illness—of course you'll be antisocial when you're depressed, dangerously cavalier when you're manic, avoidant and nervous when you're anxious. But this inability to stop pushing at the wobbly teeth of your personality, this pathological overanalyzing, doesn't stop at the bad parts—it envelopes everything. It hits the good parts in a different way, as you ask yourself whether your mental illness is actually responsible for the few traits you *like* in yourself.

"Am I truly an empathetic person? Do I really care about other people? Or am I just experiencing the pathetic recognition of a fellow loser? Am I actually outgoing and fun, or am I hopped up on mania, too brash and loud to realize how obnoxious I really am?"

Doctors talk about overidentification—where, as I discuss above, you ascribe every aspect of your character to your illness. It can be hard not to, especially if you've been ill since you were a teenager. Adolescence is a time where your sense of self begins to softly bud—and if the one thing that keeps you company throughout those years is mental illness, it's hard not to feel like it's everything you are. Who would I be without it? Which parts are me? Which parts are bipolar?

Diagnosis both helps and hinders this process. It helps in that it validates those doubts—yes, you are depressed, yes, your anxiety is real—but it doesn't quiet the other voice, the part that asks you who you'd be without your mental illness. It doesn't simplify the confused mess of mixed-up feelings, doesn't help you untangle the origin of each one, doesn't tell you where each of them should sit inside of you.

I first started seeing a therapist just after I'd dropped out of my first degree program and had been (wrongly) diagnosed with depression. He was snooty and cold and unapproachable (thus making him pretty useless as a therapist). He assigned everything I said—every fucking thing—to "self-destruction," like it was enjoyable for me to have been psychotic, to feel so desperately sad, like I had absolutely no control over my behavior whatsoever.

I remember sitting in one of our first few sessions, midway through some rant or other (and knowing me at nineteen, I was probably quoting a slightly misremembered Wikipedia-ed Camus passage or something), when he interrupted me and asked, "Don't you want to get better?"

And honestly? The answer was no.

It wasn't that I *enjoyed* being ill—clearly, obviously, I did not. I'd just had a psychotic episode in which, for two days, I had legitimately thought I was dead. I don't remember much about it, but I do know that I lay in a single bed in my tiny university room, not eating or drinking or using the bathroom, somehow convinced that I was invisible, a ghost. An actual, real-life ghost. Like Casper, if he'd spent the last year on the set of *Animal House*. It sounds really stupid; I still think about it all the time and wonder how it happened. I still desperately search for memories about it, for reasoning; what was I *thinking*? Also, what was I literally thinking?

I'm not sure about causality, but the ghost episode did correlate with a crash—the end of my first year at my university. I'd spent the entire year drinking heavily and sleeping erratically—some days for four hours, some for sixteen. My initial spurt of enthusiasm and productivity slowly trickled away and, by Christmas, I was never going to lectures. As the year wore on I became less and less social. Gone were the days when I'd go out drinking and dancing four times a week—by this point, I was never leaving my room unless it was absolutely vital. I started visiting my communal kitchen at night to ensure I would never bump into any of my housemates (more on whom later in the book). Eventually, I started ordering food online and having it delivered directly to my door, buying only things that didn't require cooking so I never, ever had to leave my room. For the two weeks before my psychotic episode began, I legitimately consumed nothing but four packets of chips a day, which I had ordered in multipack bulk. (If you were wondering: no, I still can't bear the taste of them.) I washed it all down with three 500-milliliter cans of energy drink a day, which probably didn't really help my already fractious state of mind.

My boyfriend and I had broken up a few weeks previously, a life event that *always* acts as a personal catalyst for a breakdown. It's not even that I had particularly loved him—I emphatically didn't. It was just a change in routine, a jolt. I think he could tell there was something going on, his nervous disposition betraying abject terror at my state of mind. (To add further absurdity to the situation, he had broken up with me while he was dressed as a cow.)

After the breakup, I started obsessively scanning his Facebook and Twitter accounts, trying to work out which club or pub he'd be going to that night. I'd then turn up, alone, and start talking to both him and strangers, expelling reams and reams of garbled nonsense at top speed. And when I say nonsense, I don't mean standard drunk-student fare. I mean actual gibberish, non sequiturs, sentences that tumbled out side by side despite bearing no relation to one another, words springing from my mouth in an order I couldn't predict. Most of these nights ended with me hysterical, being escorted back to my room by a bemused stranger or unsympathetic acquaintance. I often wonder what those people thought was happening—whether, as drunk eighteen-year-old freshmen, they understood that in front of them was a person unravelling. Or were they cruel behind my back, writing it off as the behavior of a "crazy bitch"? I suspect the latter, because we were all eighteen, and everyone is dumb when they're eighteen. There's more advice for friends and family later on in the book, if you want to avoid being These People.

And years before that, years before I ever touched alcohol or lived alone, and way before I was allowed to just sleep whenever I wanted, I was miserable. I self-harmed from thirteen and was suicidal from fifteen, conducting long Socratic dialogues with myself weighing the relative costs and benefits of life versus death.

I was never well-liked at school. I suspect that, to begin with, I gave off the desperate air of someone keen to be accepted, and I then morphed into a difficult, contrary girl who cared so little about being liked that aggravating people, provoking them on purpose, became a full-time hobby. Despite having light, downy blond hair, I was mocked for having hairy legs, so I deliberately and permanently stopped shaving them. Because I had listed myself as bisexual on my MySpace profile, the word "dyke" began to be hissed at me in corridors and classrooms, at which point I started writing more frequently and aggressively in notes and bulletins and blogs about my attraction to women.

But this label of "outsider" was something that I thrived on, and reveled in, and my poor mental health was an important part of that, even without a diagnosis. I was proud of it, in a way. And it was probably the main reason I was disliked, actually, rather than any of the arbitrary things that I was picked on for. I was unsettled and therefore unsettling.

I also, as teenagers do, found solace in things that reflected how I felt. I passionately loved the music of Morrissey and the Smiths, and I read and quoted and learned by rote most of Sylvia Plath's poems. I was so passionate about Morrissey that I'm pretty sure some of my old school peers probably still think of me as "that weird Morrissey girl." All very clichéd, I know this now, but those songs and poems were the center of my world, and I defined myself by them. The thread that ran through all of these passions was, obviously, misery and melancholia. It was comforting, but was it enjoyable? No. So why, then, five years later, was I telling a therapist that I didn't want to get better? It was exactly *because* of all this.

I felt like my identity was so wrapped up in my unhappiness that I wouldn't be anything without it. If I was happy, or at the very least not unhappy, there'd be nothing to me. I'd be one of those weird undressed mannequins with no head. Tabula rasa. And I would have to fill all of that up with other stuff—stuff that made me happy, I guessed, but what would that involve? Everyone's suggestions seemed arbitrary and useless—I got a job in a supermarket at my mum's behest, and it did make me more sociable and less insular, but stocking shelves does not a contented person make. What else was there? Someone suggested going back to college immediately, but my pride was still too wounded from having to drop out of my previous course to do that. Join a book club? Learn to knit? Write more? Get a boyfriend? I did all of these things, and none of them helped. They were just that—things. Without my mental illness, I felt rudderless, unmoored, lost.

My sadness in particular was something I clung onto like a security blanket; I knew it, felt safe with it, understood its subtleties and nuances in a way I never quite could with happiness. Have you ever nervously entered a room full of people you don't really know and felt so awkward that you suddenly, self-consciously, don't know what to do with your arms? That's how happiness felt to me—I couldn't quite grasp hold of it, didn't know how to support it or live beside it. It felt like an effort, an endless Sisyphean task that required faculties I didn't think I would ever possess. Do you learn to be happy? Does it just happen to you? I had no idea. Unhappiness was a known quantity. It was easier.

All of these feelings increased tenfold when I finally received my diagnosis. It was confirmation of every thought I'd ever had about "just being a naturally unhappy person," every doubt I'd ever harbored about my ability to be happy. I was right! It was all true! I wasn't exaggerating, wasn't making it up. There was *something wrong with me*, a disease not only of my brain but of my very essence.

I think some of it was performative, too. How else to deal with being called crazy all the time other than by playing up to it? It was like my resolute refusal to shave as a teenager—I'd been criticized for something, so what better way to react than by intensifying that behavior? By acting "mad," or at least by refusing to hide this madness from other people, it felt like I was proving it to them. It seems childish, and it probably is, but mad people are so rarely believed, so often dismissed, that it seemed vital for my continued existence. If people didn't know, I wouldn't know how to act at all, their inattention making me almost completely invisible. To say my behavior had been an extended "cry for help" would probably be disingenuous; it was just a cry to be heard, to say, "I am here and I am in pain." I needed it to be validated.

Diagnosis was also a huge relief because it finally allowed me to completely discard any sense of personal responsibility. I'd known I was ill for years, and sometimes, to my shame, I used it as an excuse, but I had tried to keep this to a minimum. I wanted to be sure I wasn't selling myself short or, more importantly, hurting anybody else. But as soon as I started thinking about myself so dogmatically as "a bipolar person" rather than just "Emily," things started to go a little downhill for me.

Overidentifying with my diagnosis led me to justify my bad life choices with an abandon I had never previously afforded myself. It let me act in a totally self-serving way—y'know, those things you always *want* to do but you know you can't or shouldn't. It's the perfect excuse for not being bigger or better, for not taking the positive steps you need to become the person that you really want to be. And in a way, it's childlike—safe and warm, curled up in an amniotic sac of guiltlessness. Said something stupid at work? Bipolar. Sleep with someone you probably shouldn't have? Bipolar. Flaked out on your friends because you can't be bothered to leave the house? It's not because I'm unreliable—um, *actually,* I have bipolar disorder?

It's passive, sure, but being fucked up can be a choice in itself, and it's quite often the easier one. Thinking that everything you do, good or bad, can be totally explained by your mental illness? That helps. Nobody expects anything of you; you don't expect anything of yourself. It stops the dreaded footsteps of adulthood and responsibility from encroaching on your selfish, self-indulgent plans. It is the ultimate get-out clause.

When I didn't want to think about how much I had hurt someone who cared about me, telling myself it was because I was bipolar was the only way I would deal with it. I definitely wouldn't have done it if I wasn't manic, but mania often exaggerates facets of yourself that already exist. Am I a slut or a sociopath or any of the other names that could have been justifiably thrown at me? Probably not. But I am sometimes selfish and irresponsible, and often capricious. Bipolar Emily was a caricature of me, one of those comedy portraits you get of yourself on holiday where your head is huge and you have googly eyes and a giant mouth. But cartoon or not, it was still me.

Living my life with my diagnosis tattooed on my brain, reciting it like a rosary every time I made a false move, is the single biggest mistake I've ever made. It meant I never thought about my actions, it removed my agency, it disempowered me. It made me a passive victim to my poor mental health. It should have done the opposite—I should have continued to feel as positive and enthusiastic as I did the day I first received the diagnosis. But ultimately it allowed me to absolve myself of all responsibility. Being happy isn't just a choice, of course; I have a medical illness that no amount of positive thinking or introspection can get rid of. My diagnosis was a stepping stone to working all of my shit out, and I was right in thinking it was the first step, but it wasn't some kind of magical solve-all requiring no effort on my behalf.

That's not to say that diagnosis isn't a good thing, or that it isn't a landmark point on the journey of your mental health, because it is, and it can open lots of different doors for you. We'll be exploring the ways that diagnosis can be a brilliant, life-changing thing too, later in the book. But first: how to get diagnosed in the first place.

HOW TO SUCCESSFULLY GET DIAGNOSED

So as you can see, my journey to diagnosis was long and complicated, mainly characterized by introspection. But what about the actual, tangible reality of diagnosis—the doctor's visits, the endless rote script you have to read from to be heard? How do you actually *get diagnosed?*

This is how it went for me, chronologically speaking:

- Aged fourteen, fifteen, sixteen, and seventeen—repeat visits to GP in an attempt to get depression diagnosis. Get ignored and told I'm "just a teenager."
- Aged eighteen—have full-on psychotic episode. Finally

given medication and therapy for depression. Psychosis totally ignored by doctor. Aforementioned therapist claims I'm "probably just a bit stressed."

- Aged nineteen—given free therapy on National Health Service.* It helps with my anxiety, but it only lasts six sessions, and after a while I'm back to square one.
- Aged nineteen, twenty, twenty-one—visit GP in attempt to get medication that actually does something other than make me feel worse. Get prescribed new drugs. They don't work. Go back to doctor. Get prescribed new drugs or higher doses. Repeat ad infinitum. Eventually stop taking medication.
- Aged twenty-three—second psychotic episode. Auditory and visual hallucinations. Finally see a psychiatrist who *actually asks what my symptoms are.* Finally get diagnosis, medication, and therapy that fit.

So what's the pattern here? What can you learn from nearly ten years of misdiagnosis, thoughtlessly prescribed medication, and dismissed symptoms? Sadly, it's that getting diagnosed, even being believed, can be really fucking hard.

Don't get me wrong. I've had some great experiences with deeply empathetic GPs, and with some who brusquely and

---

* In the United Kingdom, the National Health Service (NHS) is a free public health service. It's great to have access to free services, but it's not always a perfect solution.

refreshingly treat my bipolar disorder the same way they would a stomach ulcer: it's a medical fact, it's affecting your life, these are the steps we're taking to fix it. But there have been several who have been truly awful, who clearly didn't care too much about mental illness or thought I was exaggerating or a hypochondriac. After ten years of this, I now have the language to argue my point with them, but when I first started going? No way.

So what do you do when you think you're ill and you have to go and convince your doctor you need help? What do you say if they tell you to "come back in two weeks" or ask you if you've considered taking up running? Here's a guide to accessing help.

Book and Go To the Appointment

This may seem like a really, really obvious point—"to get a doctor's appointment, just book an appointment!"—but it can actually be the hardest part. Getting the courage to actually call your doctor and make an appointment is *terrifying*. But a few things to remember.

- First: the receptionist does not need to know what the appointment is about. They may ask; don't feel that you have to tell them if it makes you uncomfortable. You don't have to rush, so making sure you don't feel pressured may make a big difference in terms of your depth of discussion with your doctor and how comfortable you feel.
- Second: remember there is *absolutely no shame in asking for help if you need it.* You have not failed. You are not weak.

You are *not making it up*. What you're doing is brave and important and responsible; you're looking after yourself, loving yourself, and respecting yourself.

And yes, going to the appointment is also hard. You will probably feel nervous and have a million doubts. *What if they think I'm making it up? What if I* am *making it up? Am I a fraud? What if I make a fool of myself? What if they won't help me?* And probably more will race ad nauseum around your head.

- Third: plan in advance (see below). Take a deep breath. Take a friend to hold your hand or distract you if you need. If you're really nervous, you can take your friend into the doctor's room with you too.

Be Prepared

The key here, really, is preparation:

- Be prepared to answer certain questions ("How long have you been feeling like this?" "Do you have any desire to harm yourself?"), and have those answers ready.
- Keep a diary if you want, or even just a notebook with bullet-pointed symptoms, moods, thoughts, and behaviors. Put timestamps next to each point—there may be something significant in the timing, and having as much information as possible isn't going to hurt.
- They'll also probably ask you to fill in a survey—the

PHQ-9 (Patient Health Questionnaire)—that asks you about these feelings and how you've experienced them over the past few weeks.

You also need to be prepared for the eventuality that your doctor may obstruct your access to services. There are lots of reasons why this might happen—doctors are often stretched, and so are mental health services, so they may not want to recommend you for a service that is already overbooked. Appointments are also incredibly short—sometimes just five minutes long—and so getting across a meaningful point about your mental health in that time can be tricky. It could be, however, that you're unlucky enough to have a doctor who just doesn't take mental health as seriously as physical health. I've had a mixed bag—some incredibly understanding, some less so. Other friends have been totally incredulous at my experiences, having only come across helpful, empathetic GPs. There's no way to tell who or what you're going to get, so it's good to steel yourself just in case. Maybe this makes me a pessimist, but I like to think of myself as a completist; there is no worry I will not collect, ruminate upon, and then prepare for. There's also a database provided by the federal government that shows you where to obtain low-cost or no-cost health care, so you may be able to find alternative treatment.*

* The database to search for low-cost or no-cost health care can be accessed at http://findahealthcenter.hrsa.gov/Search_HCC.aspx.

Be prepared to feel uncomfortable and sad and maybe burst into unexpected tears at an innocuous question. Be prepared for it to be, potentially, a draining experience.

Don't feel like you have to know exactly what you want from an appointment, though. It's easy for me to say "I need to go to the doctor to change my medication," because I've been certifiably mental for ten years. I've been through it all: the nerves, the misdiagnoses, the medication, and the therapy, and the breathless, fruitless attempts to convince stony-faced doctors. You may not be at that point yet, and that is totally okay. Maybe think about what it is you're after: Do you want medication or therapy? Do you want to be diagnosed immediately, or do you want to be referred to mental health services? It's okay to not have a definite answer to any of these questions, but they are worth thinking about.

Know What You're Talking About

It's easy to feel intimidated by medical professionals, but always remember that you are the expert on your own life. You know what your symptoms are—you know how you feel. Write them down. Look them up. Self-diagnosis is often frowned upon, but it's important to understand yourself, to understand how your janky emotions or lack of coping could potentially fit into broader diagnostic spectrums.

Stand your ground

You might be lucky enough to get a good doctor who believes you and sincerely wants to help you. You might not. It can be almost impossibly hard, but try not to let them argue you into submission. You are ill. You need help. They are the gatekeeper to this help. Don't let them block access because of their own prejudices.

Don't get disheartened

One negative experience can leave a perpetual bad taste in your mouth, and I still feel dread every time I have to see a doctor about my mental health because my previous experiences have been so challenging. Don't let this happen. If one doctor doesn't help, book an appointment with a different one. Change practices. If you can, pay to see a private psychiatrist. Research local therapists—they can't diagnose you, but they can offer you advice and support throughout the process and may help you develop the emotional vocabulary to approach diagnosis again.

This can be the hardest part—the absolute despairing lows I've experienced after being knocked back by doctors have been awful. I've felt ignored, unimportant, small. It's vital that you somehow get past it in order to access help. A good thing to remember here is that *most doctors are genuinely there to help you.* You may come across someone obstinate and difficult and contrary, but the vast majority of medical staff are well-meaning and well-equipped to deal with whatever issues you have.

Remember that you are not your diagnosis

Think of yourself as one of those women you see in ads for tampons. There they are, Rollerblading and ice skating and swimming with gay abandon, not a single thought afforded to their period. Your diagnosis is the same. It cannot and will not define you.

I spoke to a recently qualified doctor friend of mine, and her advice echoes mine. Her training was comprehensive—at least eight weeks of psychiatry training including a placement, either with a hospital liaison psych team, who see referrals from other teams, or a placement in a psychiatric unit. She also did four weeks of child and adolescent psychiatry as part of her course, eight weeks of lectures in psychiatry, and four weeks in a female inpatient unit. She also elected to do an extra short course on CBT (cognitive behavioral therapy).

"We cover lots on depression, bipolar disorder, schizophrenia, and personality disorders such as borderline and schizoaffective disorder, and also cover alcohol and drug addiction," she told me. "I think there's generally a bigger focus on it now, and the importance of mental health more generally."

She agrees with me—if a doctor is being unsympathetic or unsupportive, whether because of time constraints, miscommunication, or just a poor attitude to mental health—"don't waste your mental energy on figuring out what happened." Find a new doctor—in the same practice, or another if you have to—and try again.

"Don't forget that your problems won't be solved that day," she said. "It's the beginning of a very long journey."

THE BENEFITS OF DIAGNOSIS

I've been kind of hard on diagnosis, but that's not to say that I don't think it's valuable—it is. I'm wary of the dangers of becoming completely subsumed by it, but in a practical sense, diagnosis provides a number of incredibly valuable things.

Diagnosis is the first step in accessing help. What that help might be may not be completely apparent to begin with—will you need medication, for example? Will you go to therapy? Will you be referred to other services, like a private therapist or mental health worker? Having a diagnosis makes all of this easier—and in my case, in the UK, it actually made it possible, full stop. Many mental health services in the NHS are wrapped in intractable loops of bureaucracy, and having an initial diagnosis from a GP—even if it changes later on down the line—gives you access to these services in a way that you just can't get without a referral. When I turned up at the Charing Cross Hospital Mental Health Trust sweating and weeping and close to suicide, they wanted to help me, but they couldn't actually *do* anything practical for me beyond sitting me down and talking to me and trying to calm me down. They needed a referral from my GP, which, of course, I didn't have at that point.

Having a diagnosis allows you to get to these services but also to utilize them in the most efficient way. Having a diagnosis of bipolar disorder is very different from having a diagnosis of severe anxiety, and therefore your route through the mental healthcare system will be entirely different; having a diagnosis allows you to navigate your journey to maximum advantage to you.

Diagnosis can also help you relate your condition to other people. There's much more on this later in the book, but in brief, sharing your diagnosis can be an easy way of helping people around you understand and conceptualize what you're going through. Obviously it's not always as simple as that; sometimes people have misconceptions of what particular mental illnesses mean; sometimes they'll have a whole bunch of unhelpful stereotypes whizzing around their brains. But most of the time they will not.

My experience has been generally positive. When I tell people I have bipolar disorder, they mostly understand what I mean by it. When they don't, I can explain it to them in broad terms, using both my own experience and my wider knowledge of how the condition manifests in other people.

And diagnosis can also help you understand your own condition. Even now, nearly two years after my initial diagnosis of bipolar disorder, I'm still fitting things together and understanding how patterns of behavior have affected me throughout my life. I do this mainly through the lens of, and with the help of, therapy, but sometimes things just click—I hadn't realized, for example, until about two months ago, that the general cycle of my moods actually changed with the weather. I interviewed someone with bipolar disorder—a musician I admire—and when describing how his condition manifests itself, he mentioned offhand that his cycles often correspond with the weather. When it gets warmer, he said, he's more likely to become manic.

It was only then—despite having actually lived with bipolar disorder for nearly ten years—that I realized mine did too. I sat down and thought about the timings of my psychotic episodes, my manic episodes and my depressions, and realized that it had been, broadly, the same for me. It was through discussing diagnosis—discussing a very specific condition rather than "mental health" in the abstract—that helped me on my way to this revelatory and very obvious realization.

This is the kind of conversation that diagnosis can foster—healthy, useful, and practical.

CHAPTER 2

SELF-CARE

It was three weeks into a breakdown before I made an effort to do something about it. I was constantly hearing a dial-tone that faded in and out of my head in bed, on the train, at the grocery store. Sometimes it was a barely-there whisper; at other times it would drown out almost every other noise. It started to dictate the rhythm of my conversation, the music I listened to. It had become a comfortable hum behind the dreary monotony of suicidal depression, something that actually perked my day up a bit because it felt so tangible.

Of course, it wasn't the first time I'd gone mad. It wasn't even my first "nervous breakdown," the euphemistic term my parents preferred to "psychotic episode." But it was probably the first time I was so acutely aware of the fact I was having one. Weirdly, it wasn't the auditory hallucinations or the self-harm or the countless suicide attempts that made me realize how fucked up I had become; it wasn't even the constant presence of a gaping, cavernous emptiness that sometimes crushed my chest so hard I couldn't breathe, nor the fact that, for two weeks, my diet had mainly consisted of as much booze as I could afford or stomach and one small packet of sushi a day. It was realizing how messy my apartment had become.

The floor was covered in clothes I hadn't washed in weeks and weeks, clothes I hastily sprayed with perfume before I put them back on to go to work. Everything was fetid and stale and had a sharp, musky smell that couldn't be covered by the fragrance I was trying to mask it with. I would often catch a hint of this smell in meetings or at the supermarket, and it filled me with so much shame I couldn't make eye contact with anyone and my hands would start to shake. The shame was so potent because it was imbued with the sense that this was preventable; if I had only taken that shower, this wouldn't be happening. And shouldn't taking a shower be the easiest thing in the world? Don't other people do this without thinking? It was this sense of self-rebuke that, ironically, made it even harder for me to put any of this desperate desire into action. I couldn't imagine my colleagues or friends would understand just why I couldn't spend fifteen minutes a day in the shower. *I* couldn't understand why I couldn't spend fifteen minutes a day in the shower, and that made my paralysis even worse.

I no longer had the prescience to hide the fact that my drinking was out of control. My floor was full of empty and half-empty bottles. I had become particularly fond of a cheap brand of rosé wine—I don't know how I drank it, it was so sweet and cloying.

Buying the wine became the only part of my day I would look forward to. I could never be without a bottle or two in the house, or I began to feel panicked. So every night on my way home from work, I would religiously buy two bottles, and as soon as I was home I would set about drinking them.

It went like this, without fail: I'd slam the front door behind me, dump my bags on the floor, and immediately strip, leaving the discarded clothes by the door. Then I would get into my unmade bed, still naked, and begin to drink the wine. There was no point using glasses or cups—I'd only have to wash them later, and once a fly had died at the bottom of a glass I'd left for days and I'd had to throw the whole thing away. So I would just swig from the bottle, not stopping until I passed out two hours later at around 9:00 p.m. It was kind of like when you're at university, shotgunning a bottle of bubbly wine, but with slightly fewer teenage boys dressed in bedsheet togas and slightly more existential dread.

Inevitably, I knocked over some of these bottles during nocturnal stumbles to the toilet to pee or be sick, and obviously I never bothered to mop up any of the resulting alcohol spills. As a consequence, much of the floor was gummy—and in some places fluffy from the combination of stickiness and fibers from my clothes. There were probably forty or fifty bottles of wine, beer, vodka, gin, and cider on the floor, stuffed down the side of the bed and on the windowsill. I once texted a photo of them to my best friend, a friend well aware of all of my problems and with plenty of her own, and even she was shocked.

"Fucking hell, Emily," she texted back. "Fucking hell."

Some of the bottles even had cigarette ends in them; it was so clichéd that it would have been funny if it wasn't so utterly, horribly tragic. There were unread books littering the floor too, and I found it darkly hilarious that most of them were about mental health. It looked like the set from a bad film: Sylvia Plath books next to empty bottles of vodka and packets of cigarettes. If I'd got the right filter and a good crop tool, I could even have Instagrammed it and once and for all copyrighted the Sad Girl aesthetic.

Meanwhile, blood spattered the bed to the extent that it looked like someone had been stabbed in it. It wasn't all that easy to distinguish between blood from self-harm and menstrual blood, which I had allowed to seep into the sheets. This was far better than actually buying pads or tampons. If I did that, not only would I have to leave the house, but I might actually have to look someone in the eye. Both of these scenarios were simply out of the question. I kept telling myself I would definitely change the sheets that night. I didn't. In the end my sheets were so hard with blood that I just put them in a plastic bag and threw them in a public trash can. I was too scared to put them in my building's communal Dumpster because I was convinced that someone would see them and I'd be investigated for some kind of horrible murder or satanic ritual.

It had gone on for so long that it had actually become kind of normal to me. I wasn't seeing anyone, choosing to communicate with everyone online instead of in person, so it wasn't even as though I could compare the way I was living with the clean, ordered life of someone sane. I was overcome with a kind of grim resignation that I could never be clean or functional, that this was just how it was always going to be for me. I knew it was gross and I knew it definitely wasn't "normal," but it was normal for me, and I didn't really care anyway. Even if I had, I was so paralyzed by depression, anxiety, and fear that I wouldn't have been able to do anything about it anyway.

It's not just me this happens to, either—after I finally told someone how I was living, a friend recounted a similar story. She'd wake up every morning and move all her dirty clothes, muddy shoes, and unclean plates from her bedroom floor onto her bed, telling herself that today she really would sort it out. She had to do it, or she wouldn't be able to get back into bed—right? Then, ignoring it all day, she'd eventually move it all back to the floor. This happened so often that eventually she gave up and ended up sleeping amongst this weird, unhygienic detritus for three weeks.

For her, and for me, the mess kind of represented our horrible, oppressive mental state at the time. Of course, the majority of it was plainly because we couldn't function, but there was also another element, a more meaningful psychological significance. In the same way that self-harm can be a physical expression of pain, anger, or despair, the pile of clothes in my friend's bed and the pile of bottles on my windowsill became tangible metaphors for the depths of the low we felt and how little we thought of ourselves.

The turning point came one night near Christmas, when I brought someone I was dating back to the apartment on a whim. I was a bit drunk (of course), and I had thought that the apartment was only a little bit messy. It was only when we got back that I realized how truly, horrifyingly terrible it was. I saw it all through his normal-person eyes, rather than my insane ones, and I suddenly got the horrible feeling that I might not be as okay as I had been convincing myself I was.

Panicked, I made him sit in the living room while I went into the bedroom—I think I may have even used the phrase "freshen up." What this actually meant was hastily shoving everything from the floor into my wardrobe and drawing the curtains so the gross, boozy windowsill was hidden. In the morning he innocently drew back the curtains to let the morning light in and a look of unreserved horror passed over his face. I can only imagine how he would have felt if he'd seen the terrible muddle of spilled alcohol and dirty clothes that was lying undiscovered in the wardrobe. As it was, he cleared the empty bottles for me as I sat, absolutely on fire with mortification, watching him and wishing I could either transport myself literally anywhere else or, more pressingly, be a different person entirely.

Although the date wasn't important, the way it made me feel was. It really did make me realize how abnormal and dysfunctional I had become—and when I say dysfunctional, I mean it in the most basic terms. I was simply not doing any of the things a person needs to do to survive, let alone be happy. I can't say the incident cured me, or even proved too significant a catalyst, but it definitely helped nudge me toward a mindset where I could start sorting out my life again. I didn't want to be constantly ashamed of myself or the way I lived. I wanted to be able to bring friends and partners back to my house without having to embark on a two-day operation to conceal my dirty crockery. After a shitty day at work, I wanted to be able to get into a bed that was clean and fragrant and wasn't full of empty beer bottles and blood. I wanted to actually have clean clothes.

I got better eventually. My laundry basket emptied, I threw away the rubbish. I scrubbed and Hoovered all the floors. Starting to clean my apartment is the first sign for me that my depression is lifting, the first reminder that I can be happy and capable, or at the very least that I can *cope.* But I also know that, one day, I'll find myself unwashed and exhausted amongst a pile of garbage bags. I have no doubt that it will happen again.

What the experience really illustrates to me is the huge gulf of understanding between the abstract and the actual when it comes to depression. "Depressed" is a word that has come to mean something quite different to the medical definition—it evokes something more passive than "sad" and maybe sits most closely to "melancholy." William Styron described the word as a slug that has "slithered innocuously through the language, leaving little trace of its intrinsic malevolence and preventing, by its insipidity, a general awareness of the horrible intensity of the disease when out of control." This is true both for the emotional sides of illness and the physical realities of it; but the conversation often warps the reality of actually living, day to day, with an illness.

As has been very clearly demonstrated by my own experience, depression can be fucking *disgusting.* You often hear mentions of not being able to get out of bed, or not showering for a while, or letting your room get really messy, but for me these are just comfortable euphemisms that give the reality of my life with depression a socially acceptable face. Depression is often thought of as a passive illness, characterized by lack of action, and in many ways it is. But lack of action doesn't leave you floating in a vacuum—it can leave you smelling like you live in a trashcan in an apartment that looks like a shit Tracey Emin installation from the early nineties.*

There are plenty of other examples. There have been times when my kitchen sink has heaved with multicolored mounds, and I've eaten undercooked pasta with a cheese grater as a spoon because there was neither cutlery nor a single chance that I was going to stand and wait for five more minutes to cook my dinner properly. I've not showered for days and days and days, even after sex, or on my period, or though I had to go to work. At my deepest, darkest low, a used tampon sat in a kebab box on my bedroom floor for a shameful three days before I mustered the energy, and the stomach, to throw them both in the bin. Even then, it took me a while to take the bin bag out, its smug shine mocking my inability to move for two more days. I've put perfectly good forks and knives and plates in the trash because it seemed easier than washing them. Eventually, sincerely believing I would never wash up a single thing again, I gave in and bought paper plates.

---

* Tracey Emin was a young British artist who became famous after an installation that depicted her messy, unmade bed.

Others have reported similar things to me: sleeping in beds full of blood, wearing stained and crusty clothes for weeks on end, peeing in vases or bowls or cups in their rooms to avoid going to the bathroom. One friend cried so hard she was sick, and then slept in her vomit-stained bed for four days. Mold has crept along their walls and onto their pillows, and they've slept beside empty bottles and half-eaten pizzas and dirty clothes. Once, a friend's unattended bin bag split and leaked on the floor, the juices rotting and fusing to the floor to such an extent that eventually they had to be scraped off bit by nauseating bit.

Outside of my depression, my manic episodes can often lead to the same messy results, but out of a pure lack of time more than anything else. If you spend thirteen nights out of two weeks drinking, not going home for three days at a time and taking a small mountain of drugs while you're at it, you're probably not going to be totally on top of your cleaning schedule. You probably won't have time to eat well, or really do anything that requires more than thirty-five half-arsed seconds of fleeting attention. You might be one of those people who obsessively cleans when they're manic. I am not one of those people. Like my depression, my mania involves me inadvertently making my living spaces the most disgustingly uninhabitable place they could possibly be. It's such an obsessive preoccupation for me that sometimes I feel like my whole life is a protracted piece of performance art about cultural conceptions of hygiene.

Some experiences are more extreme than others. To say this

is my normal life, or the normal life of someone else with mental health problems, would be disingenuous and reductive. Not being able to cope can be more low-key, less shockingly dramatic. Some depressed people can be perfectly functional—going to work, doing their essays at university or school, maintaining a brave face in public. But sometimes these people secretly self-harm, or just go straight to sleep as soon as they get home, or blow off their friends to sit wordlessly in the dark feeling utterly hopeless. They can't write like they used to, can't focus on work, develop drug or alcohol problems, become incapable of using public transportation. Or maybe they just feel like shit *all the time*. Despair isn't always explosive; it can be quiet and hopeless too. At these times, looking after yourself can be impossible—and this is where basic self-care comes in.

WHAT IS SELF-CARE?

Self-care is such a broad term that it can often be quite hard to define, and in many ways seems so basic and necessary to a joyful existence that it can seem like a facile thing to isolate, list, and actively attempt. What we already know, though, is that depression makes basic survival almost comically difficult.

It may sound simple and fairly obvious, but self-care works to combat the damaging effects of depression. It can be anything that makes you feel good—or at least better—in an emotional or physical sense. It's a deeply personal thing that includes "simpler" tasks such as taking a shower to larger, to more complex acts like taking part in a hobby or working for a charity. It's the stuff you do to make yourself feel fulfilled, basically. I just like to think of self-care as a means of reclaiming yourself and rediscovering your capacity for pleasure, as well as for basic acts of fulfilment.

In recent years there's been a lot of online discourse around self-care, and it is one of the best things to come out of online mental health activism. Online discourse not only gives people with mental health problems a forum to express themselves, but also provides a supportive community for those of us who find it hard to love ourselves all the time and need inspiration and help in order to care for ourselves. There are scrapbooking ideas, useful lists, blogs with links to calming noise generators and DIY face mask recipes and images full of positive affirmations. It's a great resource. Sometimes, when I'm feeling a little bit down rather than earth-shatteringly awful, even reading these lists make me feel better, regardless of whether I enact any of their suggestions or not. They add a dimension of hope to my life—the idea that I can, and will, cope.

However, there is one thing missing from this discourse: it often neglects to deal with those times when you're truly incapacitated by your mental health problems. The basic stuff: wanting to be clean, safe, and not suicidal. With this in mind, there are certain things that often come up when you research self-care. Perhaps surprisingly, considering that they are generally geared toward and written by people who have mental health problems, they actually reflect quite closely some of the suggestions most frequently heard from those without them: do some yoga, eat a healthy meal, read or recite positive affirmations, do something altruistic.

And you know what? They are definitely all true. Exercise is great, and so is eating well and being an active, engaged, positive person. They all rule, and are all great ways to maintain a healthy mind and body. But when you are truly low, this is useless advice. You're living in squalor, and you've not left your house in days. You subsist on a diet of Cheetos and lukewarm beer. There is no way you're getting out of bed, or doing three weeks' worth of laundry, and there is not a solitary hope in hell that you're going for a fucking run. Maybe when you're stable and settled and feeling okay you can start training for that 10K or totally overhauling your diet and making complicated, hundred-ingredient quinoa recipes or whatever. Often, you're not going to be able to do that when you're profoundly depressed. And that is *totally okay*. So, we also need to find strategies to help us when we feel we're almost unable to function.

SELF-CARE 101: FIFTEEN IDEAS TO HELP YOU GET YOUR SHIT TOGETHER

So you feel like shit. You're in a really sorry state. What do you do? Well, these are the most basic acts of self-care you can do, and tend mainly to physical sensations and physical safety. They're extremely rudimentary, but they're important, because whatever makes you feel good—or even just slightly less bad—is valid and meaningful and, most of all, powerful.

Open your curtains

This always makes me want to hiss like a vampire at the sunlight, but after a while it does actually make me feel more like a human being. Bonus points if you have an untidy windowsill and you tidy it up at the same time; double bonus points if you also open your window.

Get some air

Going outside for a bit is the ideal here, even if it's for five or ten minutes. But if you can't manage that—which is totally okay, by the way—then opening a window will do. Breathing in some fresh air will make you feel slightly better, and it has the benefit of making your house, apartment, or bedroom smell or feel a little fresher too.

Being able to get outside is ideal—even if you're wearing some kind of weird sweater/pajama bottoms/coat/scarf combo that makes people look at you askance—but if you can't do it then just sit by your window and breathe deeply and rejoice in the fact that your room will probably smell less like a rubbish dump when you're done.

Have a shower or bath

A lot of self-care guides tell you to focus on your shower or bath in a meditative sense—focus on the sensation of the water falling on your skin, really breathe in the scent of your soap. This can be incredibly relaxing, but for me the pleasure is mostly derived from the fact I no longer smell like a fetid pile of garbage.

If possible, use bubble bath or nice shower gel—you can get all kinds of fancy ones that cost loads, which are lovely, but cheaper things work just as well too. Lush cosmetics are kind of my go-to for this—I like to keep a bunch of their bath bombs and bubble bars in my bathroom cabinet for Emergency Sad Baths. They smell good, they make your skin feel nice, you can sit for an hour or two getting pruney and watching bad TV on your laptop. You can get things from drugstores or supermarkets too that work just as well. At the very least, it can get you through a horrible hour; at best it can feel almost transcendentally pleasurable to have warm water on your skin.

Wash your face

Nothing fancy—just some soap or some cleanser and some warm water. Again, if you can afford something more expensive, this is great, but it's more about rubbing the grime off your face.

If you're a makeup wearer who fails to remove it when you're depressed, do this. At the very least, you will look marginally more fresh, even if you don't feel it.

Get dressed

I sleep naked, so this is often a very literal step for me. But if you're set on pajamas, don't feel like you have to put on something fancy—just change from "night pajamas" to "slightly cleaner day pajamas," or put on an old T-shirt. Just change it up. I'm not sure why this works, but it really does, and several people have independently relayed back to me during the writing of this book that they have a night-pajamas-to-day-pajamas ritual when depressed, so it clearly can help.

This works extra well if you buy yourself a whole load of cheap but incredibly comfy pajamas—you can get them in big department stores or main street shops for about ten dollars a go, so a bunch of three or four pairs means you can always have something soft and nice and comfortable to wear. I always like to gift pajamas to friends when they're feeling depressed—something clean, soft, and relaxing can make the physical discomfort of being miserable a little easier to bear.

Drink a glass of water

Fun fact: many of the symptoms of dehydration resemble symptoms of anxiety or depression. You may already be experiencing dizziness, light-headedness, exhaustion, or an increased heart rate, which dehydration produces or exacerbates. Drink some water! It's not going to stop you feeling like shit, exactly, but it can help with some of the more horrible physical side effects. I also find that drinking lots of water helps keep breakouts to a minimum (yes, you still get pimples when you're twenty-five; everyone lied to me too), which also makes me feel marginally less like I'm a terrible, ugly, amorphous blob. Plus, drinking more water means getting up to pee more, so your days spent lying in bed will at least be punctuated by trips to the bathroom. Scenic!

Stretch

The best thing about this one is you don't even have to get out of bed to do it if you can't or don't want to. There are all sorts of yoga stretches you can do lying down, in your pajamas, in bed—just Google them. For me, just stretching my whole body out, stretching my arms and legs and feet, can help me feel slightly more awake and alert and alive, and can remind me that the huge lump of meat that is my currently useless body actually does have the capacity to move and feel free and joyous.

Write a to-do list

This doesn't have to be complex or full of challenging things—think of it more as a daily routine to-do list. Decide what you want to prioritize every day—getting out of bed before a certain time, having a shower, putting some clothes on—and put it on a daily to-do list. Even if you're only doing a very few very small things, ticking them off a list makes you feel productive and positive. Adding tiny, seemingly inconsequential things to my to-do list has been one of the best things I've ever done for my mental health; maybe I can't go for a run, but can I reply to one email? Yes. I've ticked off a thing. I feel more like a person who is capable of doing things.

Don't worry about the bar being set low, and **do not worry if you don't complete it.** It is a work in progress, not a set timetable, so don't worry if you can only manage one, or even none, of the things on your list. Making a list is an achievement in itself—so you've done one thing already.

Tidy your immediate surroundings

The phrase "tidy house, tidy mind" is anathema to me, considering that I'm a pretty messy person at the best of times. I will grudgingly accept that there is a small amount of truth in it, though.

When I say "try to tidy up," I don't mean doing a huge deep dive through your wardrobe and cupboards, or scrubbing things for hours and hours. What I mean is: Tidy your bedside table. Clear things off your windowsill. Get rid of the small pile of clothes at the bottom of your bed. Hang up two or three of the pieces of clothing that are on the floor. Take out the garbage. Even if what you're doing is collating the mess—putting all of your mess into one pile, for example—you're doing a good job. You're making it easier for future you—who will, as you know, absolutely be less depressed—to clear things up.

When I cleaned up five or six wine bottles out of my collection of fifty, it helped clear my mind a little bit, even though it was a tiny and insignificant dent in a much larger job. It made me realize that the task—and by extension the depressive rut I was in—was actually conquerable. It was still a disgusting mess, but it was one percent less of a disgusting mess. It helped; I felt a brief glimmer of what wasn't hope exactly, but something vaguely related to it.

Fill a bag full of garbage

Just one tiny supermarket bag will do. Chuck whatever is on the floor or in the bottom of your bag in the trash, or empty the fridge of gross, rotten food. Are there things in your drawers that you never use? Throw them away. Receipts in your wallet or your coat pockets? Throw them away. Get rid of lots of very tiny things. If you can, try to do something bigger and fill an entire garbage bag.

Smell something good

Perfume, body lotion, incense, those fancy aromatherapy oils, garlic bread. Whatever. This feels really nice on a really basic level, and is also very good for dissociation or anxiety because it physically grounds you.

If you're having a panic attack, for example, a familiar or calming smell can drag you back down to a physical reality in which you can deal slightly better with what's happening. It's all personal, of course, but some essential oils that can be good are lavender (probably smells like your grandma but is super calming), peppermint (which might invigorate you), and orange (which can also calm you down). I now have an essential oil burner, which I use when I'm down, as well as about a million scented candles—which, when I can be bothered to light them, do make me feel something other than total sensory and emotional apathy. They also look nice—especially if you're lying in the dark—which can provide an extra visual treat. (But please don't fall asleep and burn your house down.)

Eat something

It's so easy to slip into not eating when you're really down. I often fail to eat when I'm depressed because eating means either effort or money, both things in fairly short supply. I end up either drinking myself to sleep, unfed, or ordering a horrible takeout.

We all know that it's probably best to eat healthily—like stretching or washing, eating well can actually make a difference in the way that you feel emotionally and physically—but fuck it. If you're incredibly depressed and you want to order thirty dollars' worth of pizza and eat it alone in bed, then do it. The likelihood of your getting up and making a twelve-ingredient stir-fry with kale and bean sprouts is fairly low, so just make sure you're eating *something*. (Plus a slice of pizza with mushrooms on it is definitely one of your five a day.)

Move

Guides to depression always bang on about exercise, which is great when you're stable, but less so when you're so low you can barely move your head to look out of the window. Do something small; walk to the end of your road and back, or up and down some stairs a few times, or do ten jumping jacks and lie back down again. Something small and manageable that will make you feel slightly more energized but isn't superhuman.

You can even just shake your arms and legs a bit in bed, or get out of bed and walk around your room twice. You might actually find that once you've started moving, you want to carry on—it's actually propelling yourself out of inaction in the first place that's the hardest part. At the very least, getting up and moving and it being terrible means that getting back *into* bed will feel incredibly relieving.

Talk to someone

This is probably the thing that I rely on most when I'm depressed: talking to other people. This doesn't have to be a deep conversation about the state of your mental health, it can just be a really laid back chat with a friend or family member or someone online. Twitter, Reddit, and other online communities are great for this, because you're under no obligation to talk about how you are and you can just talk about Game of Thrones or sex or hummus or whatever. There are forums for pretty much anything online, and whiling away the hours talking about a thing you're interested in can be a really good way of distracting yourself from your own low mood.

If someone can come over to see you or you can bring yourself to go to meet them, even better; having someone there physically can really help. If not, a phone call or a fun and distracting WhatsApp conversation can have almost the same effect.

Breathing exercises

It might sound like bollocks, but breathing exercises really can make you calmer and more serene—which in turn can make facing the rest of the day less daunting—and are especially excellent for anxiety and panic attacks. The classic—breathing deeply in through the nose, and exhaling slowly out through the mouth, each to the count of five—generally works for me, but there is a myriad of others. A quick Google for "breathing exercises for anxiety" or "mindfulness breathing exercises" should give you a whole host of options to try so you can work out what works best for you. There are also a bunch of breathing exercises at the back of the book if you want to have a go.

Don't worry if they don't particularly help, though—I have several friends who swear that even the most focused regime of breathing exercises does nothing for them. Breathing has helped me in the past, though, so it's worth a shot.

These aren't the be-all and end-all of "getting better" (whatever that even means) but they can be a great way to get started. Why not think of some more to add to your own list? Adding them to a nice notebook can be another way of distracting yourself, doing something productive, and looking after yourself.

It's also SUPER important to remember that you're not always going to be able to do even the tiny things that you want or plan to do. If you can't manage to have a shower or get dressed, you've not failed. Try again later in the day, or tomorrow. Be patient and kind with yourself.

This is basically the real key to self-care for me: self-congratulation. I don't mean you have to throw yourself a parade every time you get out of bed, but it's easy to dismiss small achievements as meaningless. There's a tendency to write off a shower, or washing up, as "just things that normal people do," and to self-flagellate over your inability to do them on a day-to-day basis. But depression is fucking *hard.*

Not only is it emotionally hard, but it's physically draining. It saps every single ounce of willpower from your body. It makes your muscles hurt and it fucks with your sleep patterns and often renders you stupefyingly zombielike, unable to process even the simplest, most undemanding conversations. So if "all" you've done is open your curtains, then you've achieved something. Go you.

ADVANCED SELF-CARE

So: you've had your shower and got dressed, and maybe you've even started doing a little bit of exercise. You're no longer falling through an unending void of despair, and you're feeling able to look after yourself physically. So how do you deal with the emotional stuff? How do you try to maintain this level of coping and stability?

You've probably guessed it by now, but the answer is…more self-care. You need practical tactics to help you manage the transition, rather than simply promising to "love yourself" and hoping for the best (though of course a positive mindset is helpful, it's hard to sustain if you don't have anything to fall back on).

This is all about maintaining the level of stability you've probably been working on for a while, and is about more than just surviving and trying to get out of bed. With this in mind, it's important to remember that the following list is likely to be challenging in different ways—emotionally tough, or maybe just kind of boring. Getting well can be really, really boring.

Do your research

If you have a diagnosis, it can be useful to actually learn more about it. There are hundreds of books about mental illness besides this one, from memoir and biography to medical textbook and self-help, as well as innumerable blogs. The benefits are twofold: not only do you get respite from the sometimes crushing solitude of being ill and feeling like you're entirely alone, you might also understand yourself and your moods better too. There is no such thing as knowing too much about your mental health problems.

This, too, can help you develop coping strategies. During the course of your reading, you're likely to come across a bunch of different techniques from different schools of thought, or read blogs or articles by people with their own suggestions on how to get or stay well. Write them down; absolutely cannibalize every piece of information you think could possibly help you, and log them all in a notebook, journal, or online diary.

Keep a mood diary

Mood diaries are a key part of cognitive behavioral therapy, and are often used in other therapeutic programs. Their benefits are multiple: not only are you being more mindful of your actions, thoughts, and behaviors, but you're also able to notice patterns that can warn you of a potential depressive or manic episode.

They work fairly simply: you just record the time of day and how you're feeling, and can add other details such as sleep patterns, alcohol or drug consumption and diet. Establish a scale for your moods from one to ten—this might differ depending on what condition you have. If you have bipolar disorder, for example, a one may be suicidally depressed, and a ten may be manic; if you have anxiety, then one may be calm, and ten may be having a panic attack. For depression, one could again be suicidal, but ten could be feeling happy and stable.

An example is at the back of the book, or you can Google an example and print it out. I keep a mood diary in a spreadsheet on my Google Drive so I can update how I'm feeling when I'm at work or from my phone. There are also online programs and mobile apps that allow you to track your mood, but a good old-fashioned notebook can work just as well if you'd rather have something physical.

Write an "in case of emergency" list

Are you stable now? Yes. Will you be stable forever? Maybe not. So you need to prepare yourself. What are your first warning signs? Write them down (the mood diary will help). Who should you call if you start to notice them? Write their names down, write their numbers down. Be prepared. Give the list to someone else—a partner or friend or family member—and tell them what to do if you need help.

It may also help to share your mood diary—or at least a rough, edited approximation of it—with someone who you really trust. This could be a friend, a partner, or a family member whom you trust to look after you. You may not want to tell them every detail of your mood—some things are private, after all—but keeping them updated with the broad scope of your mood can help. If you're about to have a manic episode, for example, someone else may be better equipped to notice and may be able to quell problematic behavior (by taking away your credit card, for example, or ensuring that you stay in a set number of nights a week). However, this obviously all has to be done with clear, engaged, and ongoing consent, so that everybody is aware of the limits of their involvement and you're not being forced to do things that you don't really want to do or that aren't beneficial for your health.

Eat well

It's really boring, but leading a healthy lifestyle does actually help maintain good mental health. The American Mental Health Foundation suggests that whole grain foods and those containing zinc (such as meat and dairy products) and omega-3 oils (such as fish) are linked to good mental health, as is a daily intake of fresh fruit. Nuts, vegetables, and pulses (such as beans, lentils, and chickpeas) also fill you up and make you feel less tired, and low-sugar diets can help control the genuinely terrible mood swings and energy crashes caused by high sugar levels. You can also take vitamins—I take iron, vitamin C, and vitamin D tablets—if you want to boost your diet, but do check with your doctor or health professional before you start downing eighteen different multivitamins a day.

Cutting down on alcohol and caffeine is a good way of maintaining a healthier diet, as they can both exacerbate (and sometimes even trigger) periods of depression and anxiety. Caffeine is a big one for me—when I cut down, it was an almost transcendental revelation. I'd have a coffee before I got on the bus to work, then one as soon as I arrived. I'd drink tea throughout the day, and sometimes more coffee, as well as Diet Coke and sometimes energy drinks. I wondered why I felt so physically awful—I'd started exercising a little more by this point, and eating better. I'd wake up sweating and groggy and feeling as if I was about to die. But as soon as I cut down, this disappeared—I had a headache for a few days, but that was about it. Caffeine had been a huge and completely unnoticed drain on my mental and physical health.

It's not just eating *well*, as such, either. It's about eating *regularly*. Try not to skip meals; plan in advance if you have to. Try your hardest to eat fruit and vegetables and drink a bunch of water every day (again, there are apps which can help you monitor your water intake and will send you periodic push notifications on your phone to remind you to drink more). None of this stuff will ever *prevent* you from becoming ill again, but it can help maintain a feeling of general well-being, and may help you feel more stable and better equipped to deal with things.

You also, obviously, should still eat fries whenever you want.

Exercise

Again, this is one of those things people who know nothing about mental illness tell people with mental illnesses to do, and it's really fucking annoying, so I'm kind of loath to put it as a recommendation. It will not cure you. It will never, ever make you Not Ill. But it can be quite a useful coping mechanism, and as we all know by now, exercise releases all kinds of awesome neurotransmitters that can contribute to good mental health. So it's not all bullshit.

Don't do anything you're not comfortable with; don't feel like you have to go to the gym every day or run a 10K. Just do as much or as little exercise as you feel is right for you. There are fat-positive and queer-friendly gyms and workout sessions across the U.S., as well as women-only sessions and gyms. There are also a bunch of YouTube workout channels that promote body positivity without any of the damaging, patriarchal bullshit that says men and women have to look a certain way. These kinds of tutorials can be a good way to start your exercise journey because you can do them at home and you can find out what works for you in your own time. I also find it quite hard to go to the gym—once I'm there, I'm fine, if a little uncoordinated—but actually getting up, putting on gym clothes, and walking to the gym is really hard for me to do. At-home workouts are really good if you struggle with this too, because you don't have to face leaving the house.

BUT! It is very important to note that exercise is **not** a panacea for mental health problems and can actually be part of damaging behavior for some people: the obsessive counting of reps, or exercising too hard because you feel bad about your body or because you're manic. During one particularly bad manic episode, I would go to the gym twice a day, every day for about two months, and I was barely eating, either. I became absolutely fixated on how much I was working out, and how many calories I'd burned. I was ostensibly doing something good—vegetables! running!—but was inadvertently reinforcing negative behaviors.

And if someone tells you that yoga will cure your depression, you have my permission to tell them to fuck off.

Sort out your sleep

Mental illness often brings with it sleep disturbances; you sleep too much or too little, and sometimes ricochet, caffeine-addled and groggy, between the two. Practicing good sleep hygiene (habits that contribute to a normal, solid sleep) can make a huge difference to mental health, so read up on it.

Some vague pointers that have helped me and lots of my friends:

- Try not to be in bed for anything other than sex and sleeping.
- Exercise a little more—this can genuinely help your sleep.
- Reduce your caffeine intake, especially close to bedtime.
- Try—try!—to get up at the same time each morning to establish a routine—even if you're still tired. This can be incredibly hard to maintain, however, especially if you work from home or are a student, so don't get too hung up on it.

- Try not to nap during the day (which I guess goes back to the first point—don't get into bed to do anything other than fuck or fall asleep at night).
- Keep a sleep diary. Note things like the time you got into bed and what time you eventually fell asleep, add details like how much alcohol or caffeine you'd had that day and how much exercise. This may not be a short-term solution, but it may give you some clues as to what helps you and what stops you from sleeping.
- Try to make your room a nice, comfortable, comforting place to be. My bedroom is full of paintings and books and strings of fairy lights. When I get home and go into my bedroom, it's a calm, relaxing place that just *feels* soothing to be in, and makes going to sleep more pleasant than when it was full of cider bottles and unopened mail.
- Make a to-do list before bed. This may seem a little spurious, but it can actually help—I can't count the number of times I've lain in bed unable to sleep, pathologically worrying about whatever it is I have to do the next day. Writing it all down before bed—even if it's one of the very small "get up, put clothes on, wash face" self-care to-do lists—can clear your mind a little before you try to get to sleep.

It's also important to note that these kind of holistic sleep hygiene methods aren't always effective—several of my friends have tried all of these techniques with incredible enthusiasm and still found themselves unable to sleep. If this is the case, head to your GP to have a chat, because they may be able to prescribe you sleeping pills.

Go to therapy

There's a whole section dedicated to this later on in the book, but it's worth reiterating.

Therapy doesn't always work; it doesn't always make you feel good. But for lots of people, it's a vital part of staying stable and sane, and is certainly worth a try if you have things you want or need to work through. It can help provide a safe, calm space for you to talk about how you're feeling, establish warning signs and triggers, and have some respite from the rest of your (possibly stressful) life.

Join a support group

This is something a number of my friends have done, and they've found it invaluable. There's the main, and most obvious, point of having found a group of people who just wordlessly understand what you're going through. There's also increased support, a new network of people who can probably provide the most specific care you need—they've been through it themselves, after all. There's a therapeutic element to the groups too, which can either act as an initial way in to a further beneficial experience or bolster one you're already involved with.

Support groups are available across the country for a number of different mental health conditions, and groups that are specifically for young people, women, people who are LGBTQ, and more are also available, so you should be able to find somewhere you feel safe to talk through your experiences.

Set goals

What are your aims in terms of your mental health? In the short term and the long term, what do you hope to achieve? "Short term" could mean "showering at least four times a week" or "getting to bed before 1:00 a.m." "Long term" could mean "stop self-harming" or "cut down on drinking." Isolate your goals and break them down into smaller parts. Tackle each part methodically and carefully and don't worry if you have to start all over again more than once. And though it seems overwhelming, one way to achieve this is through SMART goals.

SMART Goals

Psychologists talk a lot about "SMART goals." SMART is essentially a strategy used to structure goals, and to detail a few qualities your aims should have in order for them to be achieved most successfully. They should be specific, measurable, achievable, relevant, and time-bound (hence "SMART"). Quite often, these are used for big goals like graduating or getting a promotion or something, but they can be applied to goals at both ends of the self help spectrum. I actually like to use the concept when I'm feeling horrible and feel like doing some teeny tiny acts of self-care; the example SMART goal we'll use is "having a shower," because it's probably the thing I have the biggest problem with when I'm having a bad time.

There are six questions you can ask yourself when setting one of these little goals, and luckily they all start with W, so they're easy to remember:

- **Who** is involved? (This is self-care, so just yourself. That was easy.)
- **What** do I want to accomplish? (Get undressed. Get into bathroom. Shower. Get dressed again.)
- **Where** is it? (The shower, obviously.)
- **When** do you want to do it by? (By 12:00 p.m.? By the end of the day? Whenever feels good for you is fine, as long as you set an actual time limit on what you want to do.)
- **Which** things will I need to accomplish this, and what are the constraints? (You need yourself, a towel, a shower, and some willpower. Constraints are not wanting to move or get out of bed.)
- **Why** are you doing it? (To feel clean and smell great and probably feel like 2 percent better.)

Breaking it down like this, and breaking it down even further into steps (one, sit up; two, get out of bed; three, get undressed, etc.) can make small tasks feel a lot less challenging. You've defined the parameters of your effort; you have a better idea of how much energy each step will expend. They can really give structure to your self-care and maybe make actually doing what you want or need to do a lot easier. If you know you've done four steps of a nine-step process, then you know you're already halfway to your goal. There's no nebulous dread hanging over your head, because your path is clear.

So, how can we use SMART goals to achieve a bigger challenge? In exactly the same way. Although it will take longer and may require harder work than the shower example, SMART goals are perfect for more challenging long-term goals. This time, we'll use the example of "cutting down on alcohol." This can be a vague and intimidating idea, but by making it specific, you can turn it into something much more manageable.

- **Who** is involved? As always, you're involved, but this time so are others. Let your friends and family know you're trying to cut down on alcohol, and ask them not to buy you drinks or offer you a beer or glass of wine when you're sitting watching television on the weekend. Ask them to be aware of your goal and arrange meetings in venues that don't involve alcohol, like coffee shops or the movie theater.
- **What** do you want to accomplish? We already know that you want to cut down on alcohol, but remember the "specific" part of SMART. Decide how many drinks per week you want to cut down by, or designate several days a week to be completely alcohol free.
- **Where** is it? This is less relevant, because it doesn't take

place in a particular location, but isolate the physical locations in which you're most likely to drink. At friends' houses? With work colleagues? Be mindful of these places.

- **When** do you want to do it by? Again, this is personal choice. Set a reasonable deadline for yourself to stop drinking, and go slowly. Don't be afraid to adjust your expectations—if, after a month, you're only on two alcohol-free days a week instead of the three you wanted, adjust your timeline accordingly.
- **Which** things will I need to accomplish this, and what are the constraints? Things you need: support from friends, an app or diary to track your drinking, and potentially guidance from a counselor or GP. Constraints are the desire to drink, triggering or provocative situations (dates in bars, or parties, or having a bad day).
- **Why** are you doing it? To be healthier, to develop better coping mechanisms, to lose weight, to save money—whatever the reason, note it and keep it in mind.

Sometimes, you won't be able to do anything to defend yourself against the unstoppable forces of ill mental health. Sometimes you will wake up one day and realize that you're stuck in a rabbit warren of depression. But other times, if you try to look after yourself and you pay close attention to how you feel, you can just about stop the horrible, crushing onset. If even for a minor respite, self-care is definitely worth the investment of time.

CHAPTER 3
DATING

Mental illness can be a solitary thing. What defines it above all else is introspection—the analysis of every thought and mood and whim, the endless dissection of every feeling. It boils down to the profound, secret hope of every ill person: that maybe, this time, with enough analysis, you'll find that elusive, significant key that unlocks the meaning behind all the senseless misery.

This often means that much of the literature around mental health focuses on this, too. It asks, "How do you feel?" or tells you, "It was so hard for me." Very rarely does anybody tell you how to be, not only within yourself but around other people.

When it does, there's a weird focus on love as the ultimate redemptive force, a way to thrive and recover outside of medication or therapy. Relationships—romantic or otherwise—are always the climax in these kinds of stories, the final chapter that sends you on your way with a huge dose of saccharine hope.

This isn't really how it works. Believe it or not, many people with mental illnesses have happy, healthy childhoods and cool friends and a normal social life. They have partners, spouses, children, whatever. And most importantly: the vast majority of these are pretty standard relationships. Boring, even. Very few of these people "save" you. They're just there, going out for drinks with you and watching *House of Cards* with you and texting you dinner ingredients on their way home from work. They're not cinematically charismatic people who sweep into your life with perfectly formed pieces of wisdom. They just support you quietly, sensibly, steadily.

None of those imaginary narratives actually describe very accurately how mentally ill people do relate to others, meaning that you grow up blissfully unaware of the myriad of ways that mental illness *will* affect your relationships. Please note that by relationships I mean every single one: your romantic relationships, if you have them; your friendships; and your family life.

The next few chapters will explore these relationships. How do you navigate the muddied, confused waters of relating yourself to other people? And what is it like from the other perspective? In other words: What is it like to love someone who is mentally ill, and how can you help them?

The first of these relationships to look at is one of the most awkward to navigate: dating.

Dating is hard. It's paved with heartache and unrequited crushes and blurting out gabbled nonsense in front of the unimpressed person you like. When I finally found myself in a conversation with someone I liked at work, the back of whose head I had resolutely stared at for a full three months, I answered an innocuous "So how's your day going?" with "I AM AWASH WITH EXISTENTIAL DESPAIR." She stared, confused and unblinking, back into my face. I then followed it up with a tiny, pathetic "Woo!" She sat back down. I continued to stare at the back of her head from my desk, only this time in the full knowledge she would never speak to me ever again.

This isn't just me, right? This is how it is for everyone. This is what it's like to date. It's awkward.

But what is it like when, in addition to your inability to say anything even remotely funny or good to the person you're into, you also have a mental health problem on top of it? How does that affect the way you interact with them, and how does it affect a relationship once you're actually in one? And maybe most pressingly: How do you even *tell someone* you are, or have been, ill? At what point during the dating process is it even appropriate to bring up mental health?

The pressure of not knowing when or how to let someone know your mental health status can be an additional, and very valid, source of anxiety. If you tell someone too soon, it can feel like you're setting the stakes too high, but if you leave it too long, you might unfortunately find that the person you're dating has offensive views on mental health, doesn't want to deal with it, or just isn't equipped to deal with it at all.

As a serial dater, it's something I've contended with a lot. It's also something I've done badly a lot. You would think there was a finite number of ways to do this wrong. There is not.

I still don't know how to do it; I seem to always mistime it, or phrase it badly, and I think quite often, in my haste to reassure my potential partner that it's not really a big deal, I can come across like a wide-eyed, cartoon mad person who's not only completely insane but in denial of it too. My method now is to just crowbar in the fact that I'm writing a book about mental health—the subtext is clear as soon as I say it—but most people do not have this to fall back on (though I guess the old saying goes that everybody has a book in them, and I do absolutely recommend it as an ice-breaker).

HOW *NOT* TO TELL SOMEONE YOU'RE MENTALLY ILL

Some poor ways I've handled this so far:

Completely avoided telling someone until it was catastrophically too late

Hey! I thought, after a month or two of relative tranquility. *I think maybe I don't have mental health problems anymore! I think maybe things are going to be great and perfect forever and I'm never going to have to think about this ever again! There's absolutely no point telling my new boyfriend about it, is there? Nah. It'll be fine. I'll be fine. I'm fine.*

It was not fine.

It turned out he was the kind of person who called self-harm "attention-seeking" and thought anyone with depression should "pull themselves together." After two dates, this would have been fine—I'd have just dumped him. After two months, even, I could have escaped from the relationship pretty much unscathed. After two years, though, it came as a horrifying blow, and one that precipitated the inevitable end of the relationship.

I'd kind of avoided talking about mental health with him. At that point I was deeply embarrassed by my psychotic episode, and tried to distance myself from it as much as possible. It was easier for me to avoid the topic and skirt around it awkwardly than it was for me to confront it, even to myself. I chalked up my breakdown to the stress of starting university and moving away from home and spending all my time drinking. I really didn't want to think about the possibility that this might be something that would continue to affect me for the rest of my life. Looking back, I can see why. I just wasn't emotionally equipped to deal with that idea. I was young. I wanted desperately, more than absolutely anything, to be "normal."

What this meant, in reality, wasn't actually anything even closely resembling "recovery", it was lying to myself, and everyone else, about what I wanted out of life and my relationship. It was pretending to myself that I wanted to "settle down" and live in a

1950s advertisement-esque dreamscape in which nobody is ever ill or unstable or even remotely fucked up. It also meant baking a lot of pies, which was probably the only positive to come out of the whole thing.

But, inevitably, the topic of suicide eventually came up. It was two years into the relationship, and we were in the pub. I'd had a lot of cheap red wine, and I was the kind of drunk where the world gently, nauseatingly spins and all you can taste is metal on your tongue and you're quietly spoiling for a fight. I don't remember why or how it came up, but we ended up talking about self-harm and suicide.

"It's all just attention seeking, isn't it?" he said. "It's just people who want to feel special. 'Ooh, look at me, I'm on antidepressants!' Just get on with it." He went on to tell me about an ex-girlfriend of his who had gone on antidepressants after her dad had died unexpectedly. He complained that she lay in bed all day and wouldn't have sex with him no matter how much he bugged her. It was brutal to hear him write off what was clearly a traumatic experience for her as being "lazy" and trying to "avoid sex." It was as if her depression wasn't about her at all, but was a punishment she had actively decided to enact against him. I hoped, for her sake, that he had never said these things to her, although from his tone I knew that he probably had.

It was deeply painful to hear someone I loved insult me in a way that seemed so fundamentally and unfairly personal. It was also an important moment for me because the breathtaking gut punch of the statement hit me in such a way that it forced me to consider how well I really was, and how totally instrumental my psychosis and my depression and my mania all were, in their own ways, to my self-image.

We argued about it a lot that day and from then on. He blamed me and said that he wished I would kill myself already and just get it over with if I was so serious about it. There's no doubt that he was a dickhead, and he was a dickhead in a bunch of different ways totally unrelated to my mental health, but I can't help but feel that if I had talked about my experiences earlier in the relationship, the whole thing could have been avoided.

Rule number one: it is definitely a good idea to actually, sooner or later, tell them.

Blurted it out on a first date

I was in this weird little bar, and I'd just got a great haircut, and I was on a brilliant first date. He was tall, good looking in a kind of disheveled-professor way, and the first person I'd met since the breakdown of my last relationship who had actually piqued my interest. I was very invested in not messing it up.

And I was nailing it. There was lots of wine, and I was pulling out all of my best anecdotes. Most importantly, he had TOTALLY checked out my butt when I went to the bar. So it was going pretty well, really, until this exchange:

> Him: So, you know I have a son…?
>
> Me: Oh. No. I didn't, actually.

Him: Yeah. He's ten.

Me: Don't worry about it. *I* have bipolar disorder.

So not only had I completely failed to acknowledge anything he'd just said, but I'd also compared his beloved child, the center of his universe, to a debilitating and heavily stigmatized mental health problem.

I think I felt like his child and my bipolar disorder were both things that could and would put someone off, and that he'd somehow just issued a deal-breaker amnesty by mentioning his son. In fact, he'd just wanted to tell me a boring anecdote about a trip to the zoo.

Rule number two: think before you speak (in other words, don't compare someone's child to a mental health problem on your first date).

Told someone during sex

Things you can say during sex: "That feels amazing"; "Keep doing that"; "Could you stop leaning on my hair please?" We've all read *Fifty Shades of Grey*. We know what's allowed.

Things you should not say during sex: "So, you know I have bipolar disorder?"

Don't ask me why this happened. Don't ask me about the chain of thoughts that led me to blurt it out like that.

Just remember rule number three: never say it when you are literally having sex.

Never.

HOW TO ACTUALLY TELL SOMEONE YOU'RE MENTALLY ILL IN NONE OF THE WAYS I JUST SAID

There isn't much we can actually learn from my horribly botched attempts at talking meaningfully about mental health with people I'm romantically involved with, other than "Please, god, for your own sake, do not do it in any of these ways." I think that might be because—and this is an extremely trite and predictable thing to say—every situation is so unique and nuanced that there are no hard and fast rules as to what to do. I would love to be able to say, "Yeah, you should definitely say exactly X after Y number of dates," but relationships sadly don't work like a PlayStation cheat code, as much as I wish they did. You have to play it by ear and pick up on what the person's vibe is and try to work out how best to communicate it to them.

Some tips, though:

Actually tell them

Yes, this is obvious, but it's important. I didn't tell my ex, and we saw how that went. Even if they're the understanding type, it's best to tell them before you have an episode, because you'll need to have a conversation about what you expect from them or what you might need. If they don't want to date you because they can't handle it, that's totally fine—but it's unfair to both of you if they're forced to make that decision while you're ill, and it will cause undue levels of stress.

Be honest

You don't have to tell them all the gross minutiae of your illness, but it's best to be broadly honest. Detail the type and severity of your illness. Tell them how it's affected you in the past and how it's likely to affect your relationship. Don't sugarcoat it.

Offer them some advice

Later on in this chapter there's a guide for the partners of mentally ill people. Read this list. Plagiarize the list and add to it. Give it to them, and make sure they read it. They might mess up a bit—who doesn't?—but this way they can avoid major pitfalls.

Don't be too hard on yourself

Having someone decline to date you because they decide they can't cope with your mental illness sucks. It feels deeply horrible and unavoidably personal. BUT! But! It is far better for you to be with someone who is willing and able to help you with your illness, who will look after you on the bad days as well as the good.

There's also the very valid question of whether you should even formally tell someone at all. Does putting such a strong emphasis on a diagnosis lead to an unhealthy overidentification? I'm certainly more than my bipolar disorder, so why is it even important for me to tell someone in such a stark, matter-of-fact way?

Wouldn't it be better to wait for the subject to arise naturally, if at all?

In some ways, I'm sold on this approach—you are not your illness, after all. But bipolar disorder is such a significant part of my life, whether I like it or not, that it would be strange of me to not mention it, and probably kind of irresponsible and unfair to who I'm dating. Some people can deal with mental illness; some people can't. That's fine. But I like to give them the option.

It may also cheer you to find out that a 2013 study by UK charities Mind and Relate found that 77 percent of people actively told their partners about their mental health problems, and just 5 percent of those people were broken up with because of it.* A further 74 percent of people with experience of being a partner of someone with a mental health problem said they "weren't fazed." And in the U.S. and worldwide, millions of people with mental health problems are in happy and healthy relationships. One U.S. study found that happy relationships can even improve mental health so you have almost nothing to worry about.†

---

* "People with mental health problems say partners 'not fazed' when told about their condition," last modified April 16, 2013, https://www.relate.org.uk/about-us/media-centre/press-releases/2013/12/11/people-mental-health-problems-say-partners-not-fazed-when-told-about-their-condition.

† Scott Braithwaite and Julianne Holt-Lunstad, "Romantic Relationships and Mental Health," *Current Opinion in Psychology* (February 2017): 120–125, www.sciencedirect.com/science/article/pii/S2352250X16300252.

SEX AND MENTAL HEALTH

Sexistential Crisis

According to the World Health Organization, sexual health is defined as not only "freedom from sexual diseases or disorders," but also "a capacity to enjoy and control sexual behavior without fear, shame, or guilt. A person's sexual health can be impacted by symptoms of as well as medications for mood disorders."*

The squeamish among you can breathe a sigh of relief—I'm not going to go into too much detail about my own sex life here. My mum is reading, for a start, and also there are enough gross anecdotes to fill a whole other book. What I will say, though, is that sex and mental health are, as with everything else in my entire goddamn life, linked.

The issues are twofold. One: a lack of libido. Two: far too much libido.

Lack of libido

Lack of libido is probably the less problematic of the two issues, but that's not to say it's not a big deal. Lack of libido can make you feel awful: unsexy, unattractive, guilty. It can cause relationship problems or arguments, and be the source of a not insignificant amount of self-hatred.

---

* "Sexual Health and Mood Disorders," accessed September 2016, www.dbsalliance.org/site/PageServer?pagename=education_sexual_health.

Lack of libido is a symptom of lots of mental health problems—for me, it's been most striking when I've been depressed. The study by Mind and Relate mentioned earlier found that four out of five people with mental health problems had had their sex lives affected by mental illness, with lack of libido at the top of that list.

When I'm depressed, sex is just...not a thing. I'm spending half of my energy thinking about how I wish I was dead, and the other half just trying to stay awake and alert and alive, trying to feed myself and get on the bus and not openly scream with despair at my desk. What with this packed schedule, there's just no time left for sex, and certainly no drive or energy for it. I want to lie in bed, look at the internet, eat some bad frozen pizza, and sleep. I will very occasionally masturbate, but that's about it, and it's mainly out of habit; sex just does not factor into my mental landscape. "I don't *want* to have sex, so I'm not constantly thinking 'I wish I could have sex,'" a friend told me. "What I am thinking is 'I wish I *wanted* to have sex.'" That pretty much sums it up for me.

If you have an understanding partner, your lack of libido should not be a big deal. Obviously nobody should ever pressure you into sex, make you feel guilty for not wanting to have sex, or otherwise make it an issue. That isn't a mental health issue, it's a relationship one—however you feel, however you act, nobody should *ever* coerce you or try to force your consent.

However, the fact of the matter is that a libido that becomes dramatically lower is an issue in a number of ways. Your partner may feel rejected or confused by your sudden lack of interest in sex—they might think it's something they've done. This is only natural, I think—when I've been on the other side of the whole thing, I've initially worried that it was me who was the problem, who was suddenly unsexy or unappealing. It's important, at that juncture, to reassure your partner that the problem doesn't lie with them but with you.

Explain to them that you're feeling depressed and that it's not personal to them. If you need physical space in general, tell them that it's because of how you're feeling and that you still love them. If you're still okay with nonsexual touching, then express your affection that way—but don't feel guilty if you can't.

Probably most importantly: **do not feel that you have to have sex if you don't want to.** I get the desire to please your partner, I really do. Their feelings of rejection or frustration are hard to deal with, and you might feel like they're your responsibility. **They are not your responsibility.** You are entitled to not want sex whenever you want, mental illness or not, so don't ever feel like you have to compensate to your partner for your lack of sex drive. This goes without saying for any relationship, but it's incredibly easy to lose sight of it when you're low.

Chances are it won't be your partner putting pressure on you to have sex; you'll be putting pressure on yourself. I am here to tell you not to. Relationships are about so much more than sex. They're about intimacy and trust and understanding. You'd never pressure someone else into having sex—why put yourself under the same strain?

Too much libido

The other side of it is probably less common: hypersexuality. The broadest definition of hypersexuality is frequent or suddenly increased sexual urges or activity—so wanting, or actually having, lots and lots of sex. Hypersexuality can be a problem in its own right, but it's also a side effect of several mental illnesses including bipolar disorder, borderline personality disorder, and obsessive compulsive disorder.*

Having a high sex drive is good. Having a lot of sex, if you enjoy it: also good. Regardless of your gender, if you want to go out and get it, then go out and get it. No judgment here. There is a point, however, where hypersexuality becomes a problem. When I talk about "too much libido" here, I'm not talking about kissing someone at the pub every weekend or dating a lot. I'm talking about damaging levels of sex: compulsive sex, sex you feel you have no control over. Sex as self-harm.

I'm not going to tell anyone not to engage in this kind of behavior. It would be hypocritical for one thing, and judgmental for another. There are a few things I would recommend, though:

Be responsible

Carry condoms everywhere. If you forget to use protection, then use the morning-after pill if you're able to get pregnant. Even if you

* Efforts have been made to include hypersexuality in the DSM, although, as of this writing, these efforts have failed.

have condoms, think about getting contraception you don't have to think about. The Pill is incredibly handy, but things like IUDs or the implant can remove the risk of forgetting to take it. Even if you do use implanted contraception, however, ensure that you still use condoms, have regular STI tests and encourage any regular partners to do the same.

Stay as physically safe as possible

The very nature of hypersexuality means that you might put yourself into dangerous or risky situations—normal reason can leave you as your focus narrows to sex and nothing but sex.

Always tell a friend or roommate where you're going—text them addresses of clubs or bars or people's houses. Ask them to check in on you via text or phone in the morning. Don't let your phone run out of battery; carry your phone charger with you in your bag, and get one of those portable chargers. If you see a socket and you can sit near it to look after your phone, get as much battery as possible so that you're never going to be left stranded without some way of contacting friends or calling a taxi.

Be emotionally vigilant

I know from experience that it can be incredibly easy to act upon physical compulsions without questioning them even slightly. Personally, some of that lack of questioning has been down to reticence—examining my thoughts, feelings, and behavior could potentially make me stumble across an incredibly unwanted revelation, and so I thought it best to ignore them entirely.

There are lots of reasons why someone might feel compelled to have lots of sex. It could be the intense desire for constant stimulation that often comes hand in hand with mania. It could be related to self-esteem. It could be related to past experiences. Whatever it is, and despite any potential unwillingness, it may be worth taking some time to examine the thoughts you have around your behavior.

There are also specific therapies you can undertake for issues around sex—if you Google, you should be able to find someone in your area. You might not want to stop, and that's fine, but talking it through never hurt anyone.

WHAT TO DO IF YOUR PARTNER IS MENTALLY ILL

So what if you're on the other side of all this, and you're in a relationship with someone who's mentally ill? Well, you're probably mildly terrified of messing up, and maybe you have absolutely no idea what to do. That's fine, though! It's totally fine. Nobody actually knows how to deal with it, other than by practicing—and even years of tears and fuckups and arguments don't produce a perfect, fail-safe technique.

What you actually have to contend with obviously depends

on what your partner has been diagnosed with and how their symptoms present themselves, but there are a few rules that can be adapted to pretty much any situation.

Prepare for it to sometimes be hard

We all know that no relationship is easy, regardless of the mental state of either party. Even if you're both totally stable, you will argue and get on each other's nerves.

Sometimes people fuck up really badly, but when you love someone, you forgive them.

Think of it like that, with the added caveat that they're trying really hard to not fuck up and that it isn't their fault. It's horrible to see someone you love in pain—but remember, it's probably worse for them. Be supportive.

Don't take things personally

If your partner is too depressed to have sex, or they're so anxious that they snap at you, or they're manic and they decide to go AWOL for a few days, it can be really shit. However: it's not about you. None of it is about you. When I'm panicked, I am the grouchiest, snappiest, most mean-spirited woman alive. This isn't because whoever I'm with is necessarily being a prick. It's because I am. Your partner's mental illness will sometimes hurt your feelings, sometimes make you angry, sometimes make you sick with worry, but remember: it is not your fault. It's not their fault, either. They're just struggling. Appreciate that.

That's not to say they're not responsible for their behavior. If they say something hurtful because they're depressed and lashing out, make sure you talk to them about it at a later date. Being mentally ill obviously isn't a free pass to be unapologetically mean. Chances are, though, they already know what they did wrong, and are likely to apologize anyway.

Understand what you're dealing with

Read up on your partner's diagnosis—personal accounts, medical textbooks, articles, and forums online. Talk to them about it: How do they feel when they're ill? What are their most, and least, common symptoms? Become an expert on what they're going through. Don't talk over them, explain things back to them, or profess to know more than them because you've browsed Wikipedia for an hour. Instead, quietly let them know that you're invested in your relationship and are willing to learn as much as possible to make it work.

Have a contingency plan

Know what to do in case of emergency. Ask your partner which family member or friend to contact if things get really tough. Gather resources (books, music, bubble bath, whatever) that can help calm your partner down in a crisis. Read up on and understand which local authorities you can contact if you need to. Have the number for your partner's doctor, psychiatrist, therapist, or care worker, if this is applicable or appropriate.

The most important thing here, however, is that throughout

this planning process you have the explicit consent of your partner to act on their behalf when they're ill. You need to talk carefully and extensively about what your responsibilities are as a partner, what they expect from you and at what point you would potentially be overstepping your mark in terms of their autonomy. You need to look after them, sure, but you also need to allow them to look after themselves.

Listen

This bit of advice is in almost every section of this entire book, so you're probably getting bored of it by now, but I repeat it so often because it is the single most important thing you can do to help somebody who is ill. Listen to them and what they need, and remember that they are the number one expert on their own life.

You might have worked hard to understand what they're going through, might have learned more about their diagnosis than an actual psychology student, but you should always try to defer to them and their needs. This might not always be possible—they might be delusional or in serious danger of harming themselves, in which case taking control is imperative—but most of the time, it is up to them. Quietly understand and listen to your partner, respect their wishes, and support them. That's it. Easy, really.

It may also be helpful for partners to have their own safe spaces—whether that's therapy, coffee with a friend, or a phone call with their mum—to decompress and look after themselves.

THINGS NOT TO SAY TO YOUR MENTALLY ILL PARTNER

Messing up is easy. Saying the wrong thing? Easy. A joke that falls flat, a lighthearted callback to an unresolved argument, a reference to an ex... There's a plethora of ways you can piss off your partner. This is most strikingly the case when your partner has a mental health problem that you're not sure how to deal with.

But! Never fear! I am here to save the day! Though I can't tell you exactly what to say—everyone is different, after all—I can tell you what *not* to say under any circumstances ever.

"Don't I make you happy?"

I have had so many relationships that have made me happy, with people who make me laugh, who intellectually stimulate me, who are just *so much fun*. Amazingly, though, this was not a cure for my mental illness. I still got depressed. I still had delusions. I still had auditory hallucinations. I was not magically cured, because I do not live inside a whimsical sepia-toned rom-com in which the appearance of an older man or impulsive manic pixie dream girl solves all of my problems happily and quirkily ever after.

Asking someone whether or not you make them happy essentially makes their mental illness about you. You're saying, "You have a great relationship and a nice life with me and you're still sad? What gives?" Maybe you *are* genuinely puzzled. Well, me too, buddy. It constantly puzzles me how I can have a career and partners and a great group of friends, yet still be wracked with despair on a regular basis. It makes me feel guilty and ungrateful. Don't make it worse.

Instead ask, "What can I do to make this easier for you?" It may be that the answer is "nothing," or it could turn out that you can do something practical to help—see later on in the book for some ideas on how to look after someone, or read through the chapter on self-care if you want some incredibly simple things to encourage your partner to do.

"Why don't you just go to the doctor/go for a run/eat better/other arbitrary and totally useless sentiment?"

I know, I know, this is well-meaning. It's also something that *everyone you ever talk to about mental illness* will say. Your boyfriend's sister did a Pilates course after she broke up with her boyfriend. Your girlfriend's mum told her that you should try acupuncture. All well-meaning advice that would probably work well if you were just in a rut at work or wanting to get a new hobby. But you are not. You are depressed.

It's an irritating thing to hear this from a stranger, but they don't know you after all, so you can just ignore them. When it comes from someone you love, though, it stings like a motherfucker. The implication is "You're not trying hard enough." The implication is "There are things you could be doing to make this relationship easier to handle." Even if it is well-intentioned—and in most cases it is—it isn't helpful.

If you really want to help your partner? Do the dishes maybe.

Take over the finances for a bit. Give them a hug. Buy them a nice treat. Just don't tell them to go for a fucking run.

"Is it my fault?"

Much like "don't I make you happy," asking someone if it's your fault is not going to help. Sure, if you've made a snide comment or not done something I asked you to do or forgotten to feed the cat, my bad mood is your fault. But my mental illness, which is a nebulous and inexplicable combination of genetics and biology, brain chemistry, and experience? Not really anyone's fault.

Mental illness is nobody's fault—not the person who has it or anyone around them. Ask them whether anything in particular is bothering them. Don't make it about you, because it isn't.

"I wish things could go back to how they were."

We all wish things could go back to the way they were, pal. We all wish that things were normal and stable and boring, that the biggest issue in our lives was the milk going off or something. I, too, wish that my relationships were not constantly beset by obstacles haphazardly thrown into my path by my mental illness. I, too, wish that I didn't have periods of depression in which I struggle to even vaguely recall what it feels like to laugh. I, too, wish that I didn't have manic episodes in which I hear a phone ringing in my car all night or I think that the traffic lights are secretly surveilling me. Would it be nice if I could snap out of mental illness like I do a bad mood? Yes. Would it be nice for you? Also yes. Do I want to hear about it? No. Do I want to be made to feel guilty for simply having a mental illness? *No.*

"We all get sad/anxious/overexcited sometimes..."

You're right—we do. Most people's sadness isn't pathological, though; most people are able to get out of bed most days of the week. Most people feel anxious before exams or driving tests or sometimes for no reason; not everyone literally hyperventilates at the mere thought of getting on a train or going to a party. There's a big difference between the normal spectrum of human emotions, upon which everyone is always sitting, and the experiences of someone with a mental illness.

You may think it's helpful to empathize with them—after all, you're only trying to show them that you understand what they're going through. Chances are, though, if you haven't got a mental illness, you don't. It's much better to ask them how they're feeling, to let them describe their moods and behaviors to you, and just *listen,* than to try to insert your own experience into the mix.

Dating someone when you're mentally ill can be hard on them, but it's also hard on you. There's a lingering sense that you're unlovable, that you're inherently broken in some way. Other people seem to sail through life totally unaffected by paranoia or anxiety or terrible, vicious sadness—why can't you? That's not strictly true, of course—everybody has their own shit to deal with—but when you're outside, looking in, it doesn't always seem that way.

This is what lay at the heart of my hiding my illness from my ex-boyfriend, why I buried myself inside cooking and cleaning, inside a deceptively perfect domestic life that I meticulously Instagrammed for my horrified and bemused friends. I was a television version of a normal person, desperate for it to really come true.

I've had a recurring nightmare since I was around six years old, first when I was ill, sweaty and feverish and stuck in that weird hinterland between dream and wakefulness, and then more frequently as I got older. I still have it now. In the dream I'm climbing a wall—it's one of those plastic rock-climbing walls you get in activity centers—and I know that the reason I'm endlessly crawling up this wall is because I'm reaching for something. I don't know what it is—the dream never gets that far—but there's this desperate sense of urgency, the knowledge that my goal is tantalizingly close. But for some reason I can't quite reach it.

Relationships have always felt a little like that for me. I look at other people having stable relationships and I marvel. How are they doing it? How did they reach the top of this seemingly unconquerable wall?

And who am I? I'm the ghost at the feast, the villain in a superhero movie locked inside a Plexiglass box. I'm Morrissey standing alone in a club in "How Soon Is Now?"

Even once you fall in love, it can feel just as hard. There's a line in the Netflix series *Bojack Horseman* (ostensibly a show about a talking horse but actually a dark and intelligent musing on ego, depression, and fame) where the titular character tells a girlfriend as she leaves him, "This is what always happens. You didn't know me. You fell in love with me. You got to know me." This kind of sums up the essence of how it feels to be in love when you're crazy. I have pushed many, many lovers away because of my deep-seated and unshakable belief that to be ill is to be unlovable.

Friends feel the same: "I constantly worry my boyfriend will leave me because I'm mentally ill," or "I'm always on edge because I think she's going to get sick of me." One friend told me that her relationship is the biggest source of anxiety for her during a bad episode; even though her girlfriend is supportive and always has been, the doubt niggles away at her. *Will she leave me?* she wakes up thinking. *How much longer will she put up with this? She deserves someone normal.* Of course, her girlfriend was horrified when she found out how much she'd been worrying; she loves her unconditionally, after all. Her own issues included *Am I looking after her well enough?*—which goes to show how distorted my friend's thinking was. I'm not judging her—after all, I'm exactly the same.

I've had quite a few long-term relationships since I've been an adult, and they've been largely good. I've mostly been with people who have experienced mental health problems, either first or secondhand, and who are also incredibly smart, so they've had both an intellectual and an emotional understanding of my problems. With a few exceptions, they've all dealt with my problems—in their own ways—fairly well.

The point of this story is not to show off (although I am very lucky) but to illustrate that despite this—despite the fact I've had lots of long- and short-term relationships with people who are engaging, interesting, funny, talented, and successful and who think the same of me—I still feel like my mental illness makes me an inherently unlovable person. I'm not saying that all of the fun and intimacy I've experienced with those people isn't real—the sex we've had or the in-jokes, gin-and-tonic-fueled debates on trains, or watching eight Louis Theroux documentaries in a row together—they all exist, they're all profound or fun or somewhere in between the two. What I'm saying is that mental illness has made me feel like this stuff exists on a precipice.

There's a trope in cartoons where a character is running through a seemingly endless landscape, and then suddenly smashes through a screen. The horizon isn't real, it turns out—it's fake, it's a painted TV prop. That's how I feel about being in relationships, no matter how serious or casual they are. My surroundings may be picture-perfect, but I'm patiently waiting for it all to fall down and reveal the fact that I'm in a TV studio. It's a green screen. It's a set. And the thing that will betray me, that will demolish it all, is my mental illness.

It's not true, of course. My partners have loved me unconditionally, and generally we've never bickered about anxiety or mania or depression—we've bickered about the fact that maybe they sometimes don't pick their wet towels up off the floor, or because I'm so contrary that I can start an argument, convince them of my position, and then become so annoyed they agree with me that I end the argument saying the opposite thing. These things, the things that cause friction, aren't generally because I'm mentally ill—they're because I'm a human being with flaws and quirks (and a super-annoying personality).

That's not to say my illness doesn't cause an issue in my relationships—it does, and it has in previous relationships. In some cases, I'd go so far as to say it's actively ruined them. Paranoia has been especially destructive, in that it often leads me to obsess over perceived or suspected infidelities. I lived with a boyfriend at university, and it's not an exaggeration to say we spent twenty-four hours a day together. Even if he'd wanted to cheat on me, he wouldn't have had the chance—we were inseparable. Still, my anxiety wore away at us both, making me terrified of his every blank glance at women on the street or of him being "too friendly" with a cashier. It would send me into spirals of fear and terror that took a severe toll on our relationship. Amazingly, these episodes all miraculously cleared up when I was feeling mentally healthier.

Self-harm and suicide have also loomed large over almost all of my relationships. Partners have hated seeing me hurt myself, felt powerless and impotent in its path. It's caused arguments, huge rifts, ultimatums. Others have felt unable to criticize me or break up with me in the misguided fear that I would immediately go and kill myself.

And it's made me push people away—too scared to let anyone in for fear that underneath my gregarious, outgoing exterior is a gnarled, broken person, that I'm a Russian doll that becomes uglier and more deformed as layer after layer of artifice is revealed. Why allow someone to see it? Why let someone see the real Emily—Bipolar Emily—when all it's going to do is repel them?

But it's a false dichotomy. I am bipolar. I am ill. And sometimes that manifests itself in ugly, unlovable ways. But I am also kind and empathetic, and my friends tell me I'm smart, and I always tell the best and most outrageous dinner party anecdotes. There are plenty of things to love about me, and this goes for anyone with a mental illness. The two things coexist; one doesn't cancel the other out, and nor should it. People don't love us "in spite" of our mental illness—it's just a blank, neutral fact, something that has no moral value but just…is. The "real Emily" isn't the one that I hate, or the one that I like—it's all of it, the unique jumble of happiness and sadness and mania and depression and love and any other noun you can possibly think of.

I always thought my life was predetermined, that I only had a few options in front of me. Option one: Be "cured" of my mental illness. Meet somebody and be happy and normal forever, white picket fence and all the associated regalia. Option two: accept that I'm mentally ill, but somehow get and stay well through the magical, redemptive power of love. Option three: be myself, that is to say "fully, totally mentally ill," and always be alone.

It turns out that you don't have to accept any of these options. Love can help, but it will emphatically not cure you of your mental health problems, no matter how many twee lo-fi indie films tell you that's how it works. And you don't have to be totally stable, or stable at all, to be worthy of love.

This is something I learned too late, and it is something that would have made me happier a long time ago: you can be unashamedly mentally ill and still be truly, wholly loved.

CHAPTER 4

EDUCATION

I'm not sure where the adage "your school days are the best days of your life" came from, but it's always bothered me. Throughout my childhood and adolescence, the phrase haunted me; a ratchety old specter that popped up at every desperate moment of weakness or isolation or fear. *Is this how it's supposed to feel?* I thought to myself. *Is this really the best it's going to get?*

University compounded these anxieties—wasn't I meant to be out there, having fun? Falling in love? Or even—though this was fairly unlikely—learning? I wasn't sure where "there" was, exactly, but I knew it was *somewhere.* A lyric about "dancing and laughing" from a Smiths song tormented me. I had cherished it for years, repeating it like a mantra—and, above all, secretly knowing that one day I *would* be dancing and laughing and finally living.

But I wasn't. I had the perpetual sense of someone outside looking in. It was like an endless walk home on an autumn evening—I could look inside other people's windows, look at the warmth and joy and comfort they had, but I could never get in, never play a convincing or vital part in this weird, impenetrable ceremony of normality. I felt like this every single day of my life from twelve to twenty-two—every day, near enough, floating on the periphery of something meaningful or fulfilling, never quite managing to capture or even understand the essence of what made normal people tick.

So, in short: no, my school days were not the greatest days of my life. Neither, for that matter, were my university days. And while some of my unease and unhappiness was down to being a good old-fashioned weirdo, a lot of it was to do with my latent, and later my manifest, mental health problems.

I find it slightly bizarre that people don't talk about these things more: how utterly miserable school days are written off as being a side effect of being a moody teenager; how the desperate, clawing hurt and terror and misery of being ill and alone at university are thought of as growing pains or missing home, as "failing to find your feet." I talk to friends and colleagues and the same thing crops up again and again: "I was so depressed I couldn't function" or "I dropped out because I had a nervous breakdown."

It's not just anecdotal evidence that reflects my experience; study upon study shows how many students—grade school, high school, and university—have mental health problems. A 2013 study by the National Union of Students in the UK found that 20 percent of university students consider themselves to have a mental health problem. In the U.S., a National Alliance on Mental Illness study reflected the struggles that many go through during education.* Furthermore, the Association for University and College Counseling Center Directors reports that 36.4 percent of college students experience depression in some way, but 19 percent of directors report the availability of services on the campus are inadequate.†

So why aren't we talking about it more?

Well, this chapter is my attempt to talk about it—to normalize the experience of abjectly hating school, to quiet that voice that says *maybe this is how all teenagers feel.* There are guides on how to live alone, how to survive your first weeks at college, and how to pass your exams, as well as a guide for parents who may not know how to cope with their child having problems away from home.

PRE-COLLEGE

How best to sum up my school days? Which elegantly chosen adjectives would make the list? "Boring" is definitely on there. "Unproductive" is also high on the list. But "arduous Sisyphean nightmare" probably sums it up best.

The fact was that I just didn't like myself on a pretty profound

---

* Darcy Gruttadaro and Dana Crudo, *College Students Speak: A Survey Report on Mental Health,* (Arlington: National Alliance on Mental Illness, 2012).

† Brian J. Mistler et al., *Annual Survey* (Association for University and College Counseling Center Directors, 2012).

level, and was even more profoundly unsure how I could express that. So I tried to bury it, leave it somewhere cold and dark beneath layers of uncertain narcissism, somewhere it would wither and die. But trying to ignore it made it flourish. It thrived there, in the dank gloom of my subconscious, grew stronger. It wrapped its tendrils around everything I did and especially around my throat, which would open and shut dryly, emptily. I found it hard to even speak, the weird and breathy croak escaping my mouth absolutely betraying the weirdness that was going on inside my mind.

Being unhappy at school is not a unique experience, and is one that many people live through to one degree or another. People are bullied, or they're not well-liked, or they're just awkward. But what is especially difficult is the combination of the normal, common garden-variety teenage unpleasantness and the onset of mental illness.

I don't really remember the first time I felt truly depressed. I think it probably crept up on me, no one catalyst setting me off. I remember the first time I (tried to) cut myself—more on that later—but I don't recall being particularly sad, particularly desperate, around that time. I must have been, of course, because I don't know why else I would have done it. I was too young to really know about it, and my slightly too strict mum wouldn't let me watch the kind of kid shows that dealt with "teenage issues" like self-harm. Maybe it just called to me somehow, some deep and primal desire for pain that manifested itself in a pair of blunt nail scissors. Or maybe I was just copying someone else.

But whatever the reason or whenever it started, the fact of the matter is that I was miserable all of the time. "Sad" doesn't quite capture how I felt—sad is melancholy. Sad is soft, sad is gentle, sad is looking out of a window wistfully. It's comforting in a way. What I felt was much more vicious than that, much darker. One of the diagnostic criteria of depression is "loss of interest in things you once found enjoyable," and while it's indubitably accurate, the phrase doesn't really do it justice. Depression feels like a brutal rip inside of you—this horrible clawing rawness that sucks in every ounce of joy or pleasure you can see in the world. The simple pleasures of life—a cold glass of water, a song you love, reading—are gone. In their place? Sometimes an endless chasm of ennui; sometimes a fierce and desperate rage. It is a black hole in every possible sense.

But not only was depression a viscerally horrible experience, it was confusing, too. As I got older, around fifteen, I started to piece together the way I felt and was able to tentatively connect it to the abstract concept of "depression." Before that, though, I was unmoored, with no way of understanding or conceptualizing what was happening to me. I didn't know about "mental illness" or "serotonin" or "depression" or "bipolar disorder" or even "chemical imbalance" beyond a vague recognition of what the words meant in a literal sense. These were alien ideas to me, not something I could identify with or something that I even thought about. All I knew was that every day was like a real-life version of those anxiety dreams where you're endlessly falling; there was a dark expanse below me, one that I was rapidly and haphazardly flying toward, but there was no way of stopping it.

A lot of accounts describe depression as something that happens *to* you. It's described as an animal or a monster. I saw one illustration describe it as a curse or spell. I see where these analogies are coming from, I really do. You're unutterably miserable. You don't feel yourself. You feel heavy and tired and drab. Things you previously loved have lost a shine that shows no sign of returning. You can scan your partner's face for hours, desperately searching for that impossible inch of skin that will make you feel something again. You never find it.

Even more desperately, you don't want there to be something wrong with you. "Mental illness" means doctors and pills and therapy; it means you're broken. It means that something deep and innate and inherent has gone wrong. You feel small. You feel worthless. You want to give up.

So anthropomorphizing it all seems natural. You think of depression as some snotty monster dripping bile into your brain and it seems easier. You think of a big snarling dog seated on your chest, not allowing you to move, and it seems easier. It's easier because it means something else is responsible for your misery. It's not you, after all. You're not broken. You're just temporarily weighed down by this unknowable creature.

Teenaged and miserable, this is how I came to think about my mental illness. As I said in an earlier chapter, I never thought of my sadness as being something to do with *me*. I flitted between two mindsets: (a) the idea that I was making a rational, existential choice; and (b) believing that I was a victim, someone who was being mown down by an unstoppable force that had as little to do with my sense of self as any other external energy.

It was useful to me for a while, I think, as I came to grips with what was happening to me. But in terms of getting better, and actually living with mental illness, I find the anthropomorphic approach somewhat lacking. Thinking of mental illness as something that happens *to* you absolves your responsibility; it makes you powerless. If there's a dog sitting on your chest, there's not much you can do about it. If there's a monster invading your thoughts, then what can you do? It's not about you, then, it's about the monster. Obviously, nobody thinks that there is a literal invisible dog following them around, but these abstract concepts affect the way we deal with things. Whenever I thought about how I felt, I didn't think of my depression as being anything to do with my conception of myself. Why would I? I was intelligent, engaging, a little shy, but personable and friendly. I wasn't sad. I wasn't irritable. I certainly wasn't blank, devoid of personality. These things just couldn't be me. I did nothing about it, hoping that whatever these things were, they would leave me alone again. I didn't seek help—what good would help be?

But they were *me*. They were me from thirteen to fifteen, from seventeen and well into my twenties. They were as much me as my intelligence was, my love of books, my never-an-inside-voice voice. Mental illness happens to me, sure, inasmuch as my periods of illness are temporal events, but it's also an inherent part of who I am. No big dog, no malevolent force. Just me.

That's not to say that my conceptualization of my mental illness was the only reason I didn't get help at school. There were lots of other reasons too.

A lack of appropriate vocabulary was one. Linked, in a way, to my self-imposed victimhood, I had no idea how to properly express how or what I was feeling. I channeled my frustrated energy into self-harm, a fruitless exercise that plunged me further into a cycle of self-loathing that solved exactly nothing. The secrecy of it led me to retreat further into myself, speak less and less about how I was feeling, until I became a numb shell, a conduit only for boredom and the tinny sound of Smiths songs leaked from cheap headphones. "I need help" was not a thing I knew I wanted to say. If it had been, I'm not sure I'd have known how to say it.

Once I did finally work this out, though, the next problem was actually getting people to believe what I was saying. Now that I've been through ten years' worth of mental health care, I broadly know what to ask for when I need help, and am confident enough to stand up to obstructive doctors. At school, I was not. I was desperately, desperately shy, and once I'd been told by a doctor that I was just experiencing the usual trials and tribulations of adolescence, I simply shut my mouth and refused to ask for help again.

A teacher, informed by one of my peers that I was self-harming, took me aside once—and only once—and told me I should stop. "You don't want your arms to be scarred on your wedding day, do you?" he asked. He was probably relating to me as best he could

("*Girls care about weddings, right?*") but it didn't help. He never offered help again; I never asked.

That's not to say you shouldn't tell someone—you absolutely should. My experience was particularly poor, but it's not universal. A close friend tells me that her English teacher—with whom she still keeps in touch now—was instrumental in her recovery from an eating disorder. She reached out, and it paid off; she got the help she needed, and is still recovered and happy.

HOW TO ASK FOR HELP FROM A TEACHER

It's easier for me to say "You should ask for help!" than it is for you to actually get the nerve to do it. It is indubitably scary, and it can be hard to know what to say or do, let alone what kind of help you're even asking for. Sometimes you get a shapeless, formless terror that compels you to reach out to someone, but making this terror tangible can be difficult. Nevertheless, there are a few things to keep in mind when you approach someone for help.

Arm yourself with as much information as possible

I've suggested this in almost every single chapter in the whole book, so if you're not bored of this advice, you soon will be. But, on the other hand: I am right (and it's not often I can say that with this degree of certainty). It is imperative that you have as much information as you possibly can. If you can articulate it, write down how you're feeling. Make a list if you need. Are you finding it hard to sleep, or sleeping too much? Write it down. Has there been a significant change in your appetite? Write it down. The same advice I gave for visiting GPs earlier in the book applies here.

Practice what you're going to say

If you think you're going to get nervous (as I did), then practice what you're going to say. If you have someone you can trust, practice on them. If you don't feel comfortable discussing it with a friend, then write it down or talk to yourself in the mirror. Yes, you may feel dumb, but you'll feel far less flustered in the long run. You may also just blurt it out at top speed and include none of the elegantly phrased things you had planned, but thinking it over in your head beforehand will potentially bring you the courage to do it at all.

Remember that they *want to help you*

Being a teacher is about far more than prepping students for exams; it's about providing young people with a healthy, safe, and comfortable environment in which they can thrive and grow. Looking out for the physical and mental health of students is part of the job. When my teacher tried to relate to me by asking me to think about my wedding day, he was trying to do just that. He did it badly, of course, but he still tried. The vast majority of teachers are more than happy to help you, no matter how nervous you are about telling them.

This actually leads quite neatly on to a different question: Can your teacher tell anyone else about your problems? Mine asked for my permission to call my parents and talk to them about what I'd told him (although I gave it to him, he never actually did it), though some experiences may be different. A teacher friend of mine tells me that a lot of it depends on personal discretion and the severity of the problem.*

"If a student is depressed and you offer support, it usually does involve telling the parents and safeguarding officers, but it doesn't have to," he told me. "I've had students tell me they're depressed but their parents don't know, and to pass that information on isn't necessary and is down to personal discretion."

Self-harm or suicide, however, is different—teachers are legally bound to let safeguarding officers (heads of departments, deans or principals, or support staff) know if someone is in immediate danger to themselves or others, so if you're currently suicidal or self-harming, then that information may be passed on for your own safety.

My friend also gave me some other pointers to remember from a teacher's perspective:

---

* How your teacher is able to get involved may change from state to state and school to school, so please check both state and school rules, which you should be able to find easily online. If you don't want the search to show up in your history, you can use an incognito window.

Pick your moment

If you're too nervous to organize a specific meeting, ask your teacher if you can stay behind after a lesson to talk about what you've been learning—this can give you a much safer and calmer space to discuss your mental health, and nobody will know what you actually want to talk to your teacher about. If anyone else asks, you can just tell them you're struggling with something in the lesson or wanted to double-check a note your teacher left on your homework—no need to share unless you want to.

Remember you're both totally unique and not unique at all

Teachers will absolutely have dealt with students going through similar things to you, and will have experience in the processes needed to get you help. But a good teacher will also be able to recognize that everybody's circumstances are totally unique and will need to be managed in a different way.

If they manage it well, they'll ask you for more details on how you're feeling, and will then try to help you deal with your symptoms accordingly.

It's okay to try again

If you speak to someone who couldn't—or didn't—help you, it's okay to try again! Keep trying until you find someone who can empathize and who's willing to help.

Speak up early

My friend gave me the example of a student who found presentations so anxiety-inducing that they would happily ditch lessons for a week. If this is the case, or your mental health is likely to affect you in some other way, he suggests letting your teacher know as soon as possible so they can help you manage it. They'll be able to devise strategies to help you either cope with your worries or get extra credit in a different way.

This can also apply to exams—with the right timeline, administrators or teachers might give special dispensation to students with mental health problems, or the school can take steps to ensure the exam process is as easy as possible. You probably won't get extra time—which is more for students with learning needs than emotional needs—but you may be able to apply for special consideration in terms of your score, or ask your school whether you can take the exam in a smaller room if you have anxiety, for example.

COLLEGE

I truly thought college would be different. I thought that university was the place I'd magically come into my own, somewhere I'd become the person I always wanted to be—both a magnetic femme fatale and a deeply serious thinker, someone who would hold charming and witty conversations with Capital-I Intellectuals and have a series of breathtaking love affairs with European girls with fringes and men in horn-rimmed glasses. Somehow, despite this sparkling social schedule and intense program of self-improvement, I would also graduate with the highest grades possible.

What actually happened was I spent a year getting very drunk every day, had a psychotic episode, and then spent three subsequent years hiding in my apartment, too scared to leave the house. University served to both highlight and exacerbate my mental illness, to refine it to its purest and most fucked-up peak. I had no idea what I was doing; I failed exams; I skipped lectures; I alienated everyone I met. There's no better way of describing the whole dropping-out-and-dropping-back-in-again five years than "breakdown," because my life was a terrible, broken-down mess; a nonstarting car with a horribly noxious exhaust pipe.

Of course, university or college is not a homogeneous experience. Everyone encounters unique challenges, whether in studying for or sitting exams, romantic relationships, or just day-to-day coping. And sometimes you won't even know about your mental health problems until you get there. My own, although pretty well established, took on a different form at university—this weird, shifting entity that was entirely new and unknowable. I knew I was depressed, of course, but university was the first time I ever had what I now know as a manic episode.

Mainly because I had been so ostracized at school, university seemed to me to be a good place to start over. I had a few good qualities; I was empathetic, I was funny, I was smart. Surely I could take these qualities and get rid of all the background noise? I didn't have to be this awkward, insecure person my whole life, did I?

I later found out that I didn't (I'm certainly not that person now), but what I didn't realize at the time was that the way to have people like you—really like you—is to actually be yourself. Obviously, not everyone will like you, but that's not the point—the people who like you like you because you are good, and because of that peculiar mixture of likes and dislikes you have, for your smell and your taste in books and the way you open your mouth slightly witlessly when you're thinking. I did not know this. "Be yourself" seemed like a trite and facile self-help mantra. It just didn't seem possible—it actually seemed like some kind of joke.

What I thought would be a good idea was to pretend to be an entirely different person altogether. The last version of me hadn't worked, so why not try a new one? Nobody at university would have to know what I was like before. They didn't know I had bad hair or that my personalized MySpace URL was */ilovestephenfry*. I would be cool, interesting, aloof. I would, most importantly, be popular.

I dutifully dyed my hair peroxide blond and bought a new set of clothes: the kind of clothes other girls wore, rather than the Doc Martens and band T-shirts I had got used to hiding myself in. (There was nothing wrong with these things, of course, nothing wrong with being gym-obsessed and thin and provocative in my dress, other than the fact it wasn't me.) I stopped listening to the music I liked and pretended to agree with everyone else. This meant no more arguments about queer politics and feminism. No—instead, I would be *agreeable*. I would *acquiesce*. I would exercise *restraint* and *self-control* and all of those things that make you much smaller but altogether more palatable.

Most significantly, I started going out. A lot.

There are lots of things shy people don't like. Crowds. Small talk. Getting into the lift with someone you kind-of-but-don't-quite know well enough for it to not be awkward. Sitting smugly at the top of this list is the common thread that haunts an introvert's life: socializing.

Socializing is hard. It's boring. It's thankless, mostly. It's endless small talk with people you barely know and definitely don't like; it's forcing yourself to appear happy or jolly or interested in what they have to say. It's insecurity, hoping that someone likes you but sensing that they don't. It's saying the wrong thing and painfully receiving a blank and awkward response from your conversational partner. It can make you feel small, but is also inescapably perched on the edge of a precipice that promises you the golden chalice of popularity.

And when I was eighteen, I was shy. I was incredibly shy. I was also a year ahead at school, which meant I turned eighteen only days before my first night at university. My school peers had been going out for a full year, drinking in clubs and bars and pubs. I was too much of a chicken to get a fake ID and did most of my drinking in my best friend's bedroom anyway, so "going out" as a concept was pretty alien to me. Going out, of course, is a fairly integral part of your first few weeks of university, whether you can drink legally or not. Get it right, I thought, and I would be guaranteed social success for the rest of time. Get it wrong and I would be the friendless loser I had been for the last five years. Getting it right seemed very, very important.

Your first week is every university anxiety writ large: meeting new people, navigating a new place, living alone for the first time. Add to that drinking, and sometimes drugs, and you have yourself a pretty potent and overwhelming mix, mental illness or not.

When I got to university, I started drinking in in a way I had never drunk before. The most intoxicated I had managed to get up until that point was my first ever drinking experience—New Year's Eve at my best friend's parents' house. I drank two glasses of eggnog, three glasses of champagne, and a few shots of chocolate vodka, and promptly vomited. Not in the toilet, of course, but in the sink, the laundry basket, the bed, and the floor. Great stuff.

University introduced to me subtle new nuances to the experience of being sick. It was mostly in the toilet, luckily, but it was also on a thrice-daily basis. First, a wave of nausea would hit me at around 6:00 a.m., when I would blindly stumble to my bathroom to throw up. Dry-mouthed and anxious, I would fall back into a fitful sleep before lunch, when I would eat a sandwich and promptly throw it back up. On a good day, I had drunk little enough that I could avoid this midafternoon session. My final trip to the toilet would be in the evening, after I had got back in from a night out. If I was particularly unlucky, this nocturnal ritual would start before I had left the pub or club. Occasionally, I would make myself sick on purpose, a delightful new addition to the process. If I felt a bit ill before I went out, for example, I would make myself sick—what was eloquently termed, in the early 2010s, the "tactical chunder." I could then brush my teeth and get on with the rest of the night's drinking, the taste of vomit only slightly tainting my evening and my breath.

I was also drinking throughout the day. A pint in the morning, hair of the dog, to start me off. Then slowly my drink of choice would get heavier—a gin and tonic with lunch, and then another before an afternoon nap. The drinking proper would start before I went out, though; shot after shot of sickly sweet vodka schnapps, a bottle of wine. As term went on, this drinking ritual became private. No more did I grace my apartment's kitchen with my presence—there was drinking to be done, and it had to be done quickly and efficiently. I started nailing straight spirits instead of schnapps—two fingers of vodka mixed with lemonade became three or four fingers, downed from an unclean glass. Drinking wasn't about fun anymore, it was about being drunk. The effort of maintaining this happy, carefree personality was starting to take its toll, and being drunk was the only time I felt comfortable. Deep down, I hated the entire rigmarole—getting dressed up, talking to new people. What was it for? It was empty, and so was I—the good parts of my personality had vanished along with my crusty Doc Martens.

I imagine I was hard to live with during this period. It was indubitably weird behavior that got weirder as the year went on: never leaving my room; only using the kitchen at 3:00 a.m.; posting weird photos of myself on Facebook at 4:00 a.m. It was probably a nightmare. But living with my roommates was a nightmare for me too; constantly judging me, they finally dealt with my mental health problems by coming to tell me that they didn't want to live with me after all. I don't blame them, really. Who, at nineteen, knows how to deal with that level of mania?

By the time I went back after Christmas, my mania was in full swing. It was the first real manic episode I had ever had, and I had no idea what was happening. I felt compelled to go to lectures and make notes, but when I read them back none of them seemed to make sense. I would send literally hundreds and hundreds of tweets a day, talking nonsense to celebrities and civilians alike, documenting my day in excruciating detail. I would log when my leg felt itchy or I had a small headache, or when someone walked into the courtyard of my building. I tweeted every song I listened to, and my feelings on my roommates, my course, myself, and my boyfriend were all broadcast to an increasingly large, and probably horrified, audience. I didn't think to censor my thoughts, because it felt so absolutely vital to record them. It was compulsive. People still ask me how I've managed to write forty thousand tweets—here's your answer.

My psychotic episode didn't feel like anything when it happened; it just felt normal. Now I'm older, I can sense when I'm likely to become delusional and swiftly text my best friend "I don't feel well." And I often don't. I feel out of sorts before a psychotic episode comes on, just slightly disturbed in a way I have tried and failed many times to describe. Something just feels off. I just didn't have that level of insight the first time it happened, didn't have the vocabulary to explain exactly how unsettled I felt.

Buoyed by mania, my behavior had become ever more erratic. Then, as I feel I have typed a million times, came the inevitable crash. I was suicidal.

I started self-harming in earnest again, brazenly displaying the scars to every horrified onlooker I could find, as if a reaction or an acknowledgment would validate the pain I was feeling and thus mitigate it somehow. At my most desperate, I cut my arms from my wrist to my shoulder and went to get help from a housemate. Nobody was in, so I slid down the corridor wall, utterly trapped by my own misery. When a roommate finally returned home and saw me there, covered in blood and clearly in distress, she simply stepped over my prone body and retreated to her own room. She locked the door.

Empathy can't—or shouldn't—be limitless. There's a point at which you really should stop making excuses for other people's shitty actions. And despite my particularly bad habit of reaching that point far, far too late, this was too awful for even me to excuse.

I understand I was probably difficult to live with. I understand that watching someone go from fun, outgoing friend to psychotic hermit was probably confusing, difficult, and almost definitely incredibly scary. Being confronted with something like that, especially for the first time in your life, can be truly terrifying. It's why people often say the wrong thing, why they don't understand that you can't just "pull yourself together" or why they chummily tell you to cheer up. There's a difference, though, between clueless, ignorant misunderstanding and maliciousness. It's a spectrum, of course. On one end is someone who totally gets it, who always uses the correct terminology and offers you the absolute perfect support. Hardly anybody is there—not even me, most of the time. The other end—the malicious end—is where my housemate sat.

I don't even know if I could give anyone advice, put in the same situation as I was that day. "Take care when choosing your roommates" might work later on in life, but it's pointless if we're talking about college, because happy first-year living is so dependent on the luck of the draw. Saying "ignore it" is all well and good, but it was too hurtful to ignore, too viscerally horrible to repress. It's stuck with me for five years, popping into my head at bizarre and unrelated moments—at night, when I'm drifting off to sleep, but also on the bus or at work and once, improbably, during sex. Lots of traumas—condensed down to anecdote, folded away neatly to fit a narrative—lose their edge. This hasn't. I still cannot believe that it happened; it still seems bizarre and preposterous and ridiculous to me. It seems like some kind of weird metaphor that would be considered far too broad in fiction. Surely she can't have just *stepped over me*? Surely it can't have happened the way I remember it happening? But it did.

She may not even remember it—I doubt the incident is seared into her psyche as deeply as it is mine. What I do hope is that if she does remember it, or if in the unlikely event that she reads this book and it jogs her memory, she'll be ashamed of herself. To call an ambulance or another friend—or just to sit down next to me and say "Are you okay?"—would have required very little effort. "Are you okay?" may seem meaningless to the person asking, especially if they don't really care what the answer is, but it would have been *something*. It would have been a gesture, a token nod toward the fact that I absolutely was not okay and that I needed to do something about it. To do nothing—not even that—is fairly unforgivable, in my eyes.

There's no way to say what it was about university that made me lose my mind so utterly. Alcohol didn't help, especially as it was my first experience of it, and my tolerance—now worryingly high—was close to zero. Sleeping all day and staying up all night was definitely a factor, and the stress of lectures, exams, and socializing, the triumvirate of a successful university experience, weighed heavily on me.

Mainly, though, it was just being on my own and not knowing what to do or think. I had somewhat successfully distracted myself at school; there were always lessons I had to go to, homework to be done, exams to study for. College gives you this huge expanse of unscheduled time in which you can be productive, in which I was meant to achieve the things that I had the capacity and potential to do. Unscheduled time means you have to be in your own company, though; you have to live inside your own head for hours or days at a time. It wasn't that I didn't know how to live alone, or to live with others—it was that I didn't know how to live with myself.

A BEGINNER'S GUIDE TO SURVIVING COLLEGE

So having seen how it can easily go so wrong, how do you make it go right? Or, at least, how do you make it go less wrong than me?

Remember, you don't have to drink

A table full of playing cards and empty bottles and nervous, giddy young people secretly desperate to impress each other is one of the most enduring images in the first few weeks of college. Drinking games are par for the course. There are lots of them, all designed to get you as drunk as possible as quickly as possible, and occasionally to humiliate you in front of new people while you're at it. I'm sure they have their appeal, although I've never quite seen it.

The point is, alcohol can have a serious effect on mental health. It can exacerbate depression or heighten feelings of mania; hangovers can induce anxiety attacks that feel like someone is physically squeezing your heart over and over again while you endlessly mentally replay whatever dumb thing you said the night before. If you know alcohol has this kind of effect on you and your mental health, or if you're worried about what a whole week of poor sleep, bad diet, and excessive alcohol will do for you, then *do not feel like you have to drink.*

There are lots of reasons why someone might not drink, and plenty of fake excuses if you (understandably) don't want to share your mental health worries with your new dorm neighbors or roommates. You could tell them that you're on antibiotics and you have to be careful what you drink, or that you have an incredibly important job interview in the morning. Tell people you don't feel very well, or surreptitiously make your alcohol/mixer ratio incrementally smaller as the night goes on. If you're at the bar, just get a coke or a lemonade—how is anyone else meant to know whether or not it has vodka or gin in it?

You could also allocate certain days of the week to sobriety. Drinking at college is sometimes less of a lifestyle choice and more of a necessity, as if some kind of unseen decree has decided you must exceed a certain amount of alcohol a day. It's therefore not just the nights out that get you; it's that "one drink" on a quiet night, it's the post-lecture pint or the pre-drinks you go to even if you're not going out. Try to cut back on this kind of casual non-drinking drinking. You never really *think* of this as drinking, because why would you? "Drinking" is getting blackout drunk; "drinking" is downing those sickly sweet fluorescent cocktails until you pass out. But drinking here and there adds up too—so if you can't avoid nights out, then cut down here. Have a glass of Diet Coke instead of a pint of beer after your lecture; drink one beer instead of four when you're alone in your room watching Netflix.

I'd love to say "try to have the confidence to just say no"—and if you do have that confidence, then that's great—but I've been to university more than once, and I know that "just saying no" is often a really pointless piece of advice. Do what you gotta do.

Keep in touch with friends and family

It's always a nice feeling when you turn up to the dorms on your first day of college and your roommate doesn't appear to be completely intimidating. They seem nice! It's unlikely that they're going to murder me as I sleep! I'm probably not even going to be that annoyed when they "borrow" food from my cupboard! This is amazing! It can be easy to form incredibly intense bonds with your new roommate and classmates as soon as you get to college.

It's great. I'm not saying it's not great. Many people go on to form lifelong friendships with people they meet at college. It can be difficult to predict which of these brand-new best friends is going to stick, though—that perennial friendship may not even emerge until you're in your last year. You may have lots of friends to begin with, but those friendships are often shallow and based more on convenience and insecurity than they are on a genuine connection. Talking about your mental health with these people is not always an option.

You may also feel like your mental health is something to be ashamed of, something that could put off potential friends. It's not, obviously. We all know that, really. But I found that feeling hard to shake when I went to university, and so I never talked about it. And, as we have seen, that did not end up going well for me.

So keep in touch with your existing friends and family, no matter how busy you are or how bowled over by new friends and new experiences. Communicate how you feel to them; tell them about the tiny embarrassments and the big fuckups and the ebb and flow of your moods. Schedule regular calls—this way you can tell them what's going on with you, and you'll have something to look forward to. Things like Skype, Facebook chat, and WhatsApp make it easier than ever to keep in touch with your friends—they know you *so well*, and knowing that you have that support network, no matter how far away, can really, really help.

Remember that college is not a homogeneous experience

Your friends may have gone to college and loved it. Maybe your older siblings thrived. They joined teams and went drinking; they lived with their first-year dormmates for the remainder of their degree, friends they still see now. That doesn't mean you will have, or should have, the same experience.

Mentally ill or not, everybody has a different experience of college. We're sold this glitzy idea of college being this super-fun place where everybody has a brilliant time, and that's just not the case for lots of people. Lots of people fucking *hate it*.

It may feel like you're missing out—you're not. Find the things you enjoy and do them. Who cares what everybody else is doing? Joyfully and carelessly being yourself is one of the purest forms of pleasure you can have in life. Start early.

How to live alone for the first time

Perhaps the worst part of going to university for me was living alone for the first time. As with many college-related things, the very real challenge of living alone is couched in jokes and euphemism—"Students have no idea how to boil a pan of water!" and "Taking your laundry home to your mum, eh?" may seem like playful riffs on filthy student life, but were actually incredibly pertinent predictions on how poorly I would cope alone.

I wasn't particularly spoiled as a child; I come from a comfortable background, but was expected to do chores and had a regular job before I left home. I cooked a bit—not every night, but I had a few dishes I could knock up quickly and proficiently that me and my mum would share. My room was fairly tidy, too—it wasn't minimalistic by any stretch of the imagination, but compared to friends' rooms, which were often carpeted with dirty plates and clothes, I was pretty neat. I was not a student cliché. In fact, I'd go so far as to say I was vaguely self-sufficient.

So what followed when I went to university was fairly surprising. It actually started off okay; I would cook the same three-ingredient dish (pasta, tuna, cheese) at least three times a week, but at least I was actually cooking. I did my washing up—a bit sloppily maybe, but I did it. I kept my room relatively in order, my clothes clean, my bedding fresh. And then depression hit.

As you may have already seen from the self-care chapter, my ability to remain on top of day-to-day chores when depressed is lacking. If I'm depressed, I can do nothing. And so it was at university. The plates piled up. My bedding remained unchanged. My wardrobe became a pit of dirty laundry and muddy shoes. Going to the laundry room—which was housed in a small building at least three minutes away from my room—was impossible. In the end, I got washing detergent and a kettle and washed my clothes by hand in the sink when I needed them. Instead of tumble-drying them, as my saner housemates would do, I then hung them up on the back of my door and dried them with a hairdryer. This *seemed* incredibly resourceful. It *seemed* like the best idea anyone had EVER HAD. It was not. It really, really was not.

The worse this weird mess got, the harder it was to make a dent in the tidying, and the more incapable I became of doing anything about it. So here are a few tips on how to successfully live alone, and how to deal with things if they get to be too much.

Practice before you leave home

There are certain things you can prepare for before you leave home: cooking, for one. Learn to make a few staple, healthy meals before you go—things like stir-fries, omelets, and pasta dishes. Not only are these things cheap, but they're not terrible for you and—maybe most importantly—you can make them with minimal dirty dishes. Try to get into a routine of tidying, cleaning, and cooking for yourself before you leave. Which leads us to…

Make, and stick to, tiny household goals

If you're anything like me, you'll let everything pile up until it's a huge, unmanageable mess. If you can, try to make sure this doesn't happen.

Before you get depressed, or before you realize you're overwhelmed and can't cope, put small and manageable systems into place. Make tidying a habit, and be strict with yourself. Make your bed every day. Put bleach down the toilet every other day. Get a laundry hamper and put dirty clothes into that at the end of every day, instead of on the floor. A study from University College London* found that it takes about sixty-six days to form a habit—which, in the long run, is nothing.

It may be tedious as hell, it may be boring and a little bit tiring and kind of annoying. But it is so, so much easier than dealing with a huge pile of dirty dishes and a gross, crusty toilet and a messy bed all at once.

Think of practical solutions to major problems

There is no avoiding things piling up sometimes; no matter how hard you try, if you're severely depressed, you're going to be less able to cope. And that's *totally fine.* If you have a series of practical solutions to the biggest obstructions, though, they can be a lot easier to deal with.

If you have a problem washing your dishes after eating, use paper plates. Use tin foil instead of having to wash a baking pan every time you cook. Buy frozen meals if you have to. Lots of grocery stores have relatively healthy and cheap microwave meals now, and you can buy vegetables that steam in the bag in the microwave too. There will be a practical life-hack solution to anything

---

* "How Long Does It Take to Form a Habit?", UCL News, published August 4, 2009, https://www.ucl.ac.uk/news/news-articles/0908/09080401.

you have a problem with. Try to plan ahead, and think of solutions before you need them.

Stock up

Before you go to college, or when you first arrive, stock up on the practical things you may need. I often found that inspiration to finally clean and sort my life out came at 3:00 a.m.—but if I didn't have the things I needed, then I'd go to bed again and not have another spike of energy for weeks.

There are lots of websites that detail long lists of "student essentials"—have a look and see if you can stock up on things. You're probably not going to need a pizza cutter or an egg poacher when you're depressed, but having a small supply of things like bleach, sponges, and microwave meals for when you start getting low can be really useful.

Try to stay in control of your finances

This is a biggie. I got into a lot—a lot—of debt when I was away from home the first time, debt it took me years to pay off again. This kind of thing can spiral out of control when you're depressed or manic, because buying things either seems like something that might cheer you up a bit or, at your manic worst, will be a compulsion.

This is the very most boring piece of advice of all but maybe one of the most important—try to keep on top of your finances. Make a weekly budget—how much you want to spend on food, alcohol, transport, clothes, whatever. Stick to it where you can. At the very least, track it. This can make a big difference when it comes to keeping hold of your money.

A BEGINNER'S GUIDE TO PASSING YOUR EXAMS

When Nietzsche said, "Time itself is a circle," I'm fairly sure that what he was referring to was not the idea that the universe itself is an ouroboros of time and experience and expression, but the inevitability of exams. Finals generally loom twice yearly from ages fourteen to twenty-three, a perpetual presence that manages to taint almost every moment of pure joy. Having fun with your friends? Bad luck, you've just remembered you have to take your SATs in six months. At a party? Exams. Remember the exams you have to take. Christmas Day is all well and good, but shouldn't you be studying for finals? Just got out of your final exam? Relief flooding your body like a burst dam full of hopes and dreams and new horizons? Yeah, fine, but also you'll be getting your results soon, so you better nip that one in the bud.

It's a self-evident fact that nobody likes exams, but as with all things, mental illness makes this dislike a lot more pressing and urgent. I've had mixed luck with exams. If I'm depressed, then there's no chance I'll do well, because I'll be too listless and miserable and lethargic to bother reviewing; if I'm manic, then I'll become astonishingly blasé about the exam's importance, and grossly overestimate how little I actually know and underestimate how important it is.

As such, my exam success has fluctuated dramatically, and largely been down to luck. I happened to be depressed during the first set of important exams I had when I was fifteen, and I consequently underperformed by quite a staggering degree, but when I was eighteen and on medication, I had a far better state of mind and was able to absolutely nail my exams and get into a good college. My various stints at university followed the same pattern; in my first year, on the cusp of a psychotic episode, I didn't study at all and instead went into my Philosophy of Science exam completely unprepared, eventually writing eight pages about Woody Allen, whose films I had never actually watched.

I did not pass the exam.

Later, on my final attempt at actually getting a degree, I managed to scrape by—but only just. It's a source of constant frustration; I like to think I'm intelligent, and I'm certainly engaged and interested in learning, but my mental health problems have always got in the way of demonstrating that in any tangible way. As I have repeated endlessly in this chapter, I wish I had received some support or guidance in terms of learning, especially during exam season.

I don't want to focus too much on the idea that exams mean nothing. I never did particularly well in mine, and my life has turned out all right, but one solitary example will not make you feel any less anxious about underperforming. Whether it's ACTs, SATs, or final-year college exams, you rightly want to do well, and tales of my own failure will do absolutely nothing to temper that desire. So, instead, here are some tips to help you get through your exams.

Have some perspective

Yeah, yeah, I know I just said that I wasn't going to tell you exams are meaningless, but it's my book and I'll contradict myself if I want to. Obviously exams mean *something*—they mean the key to a certain university or a particular job, or maybe your family has put you under a lot of pressure to succeed. And that's fine—in fact, it's important. If they didn't mean something, then why would you bother at all?

Meaning something doesn't make them *everything*, though. Failing an exam, or not quite hitting the grade that you wanted, feels shitty. Oh man, does it feel shitty. But you can, and you will, pick yourself up afterward and carry on. Maybe you'll adjust your plans, or maybe you'll retake the exam. Maybe you'll realize that what you wanted to do is not what you are actually suited to do. But what you will definitely do is survive. You will get to where you want to be. You will be okay.

Prepare far, far in advance

No matter how early you start studying or preparing to review, there is always that one guy who's like "I started studying, like, three months ago? But no, I totally don't know anything at all, I'm definitely going to fail." He always hogs the library books. He's always been studying for longer than everyone else. Ignore that guy. But also, maybe, take a few cues from that guy.

If you know you're likely to be struck by a period of poor mental health, prepare yourself well in advance. Make flashcards or notes before you really need to. Organize your files while you still can. Record yourself reading out said notes so you can listen to them when you're too low to even concentrate on reading. Tiny things that can seem time-consuming and pointless in advance, but are invaluable when you're not coping.

Similarly, preparing in advance can help with close-to-exam anxiety. Universities are often huge and hard to navigate, so find out what room your exam is in and visit it beforehand. Anxiety often focuses on small things like this—"will I get there on time?"—rather than the larger, more tangible worries such as actually passing the exam, so knowing exactly where you're going and how long it will take can alleviate some of this extra worry. Likewise, make sure you're prepared with the physical things you need for an exam way before exam season starts: calculators or pencils or pens or whatever. Buy them. Keep them somewhere safe. Don't leave it until the last minute.

Communicate your need for help

As already documented, asking for help can be hard. Knowing what to say and when to say it, knowing what to ask for—it's all incredibly difficult. But communicating that you need help, now or in the future, is incredibly important. Tell teachers or lecturers that you're struggling with mental illness. Tell your doctor that you're about to take exams.

Many schools and colleges take this kind of thing into consideration—colleges especially, as they can be far more flexible with when exams are given. Support may not be appropriate or adequate—many institutions fail at providing adequate care—but it may provide you with a little respite or make you feel less panicked about the prospect of taking your exams.

You may also be able to get counseling through your college health service, and many colleges have "Nightlines," phone services you can call when you're feeling depressed or under pressure. Everyone operating these services will be well trained regarding things like exams, so they may be able to offer some genuine, practical advice or tangible help around exams season.

Contact your student welfare teams, which may exist either campus-wide or within subjects and dorms—many have online resources, which can be invaluable, and you can contact them online too. You can also make appointments to see welfare staff, who may be able to point you in the right direction in terms of counseling, stress management, diet, and more.

Retakes are your friend

Once you get past high school, retakes are most definitely your friend. You can retake SATs, and you can sometimes retake college exams if your professor allows. You can sometimes retake full years of high school if that is an option you would like to consider, or go back to school to take any level of exam again. Your first go is not your only chance for success. Think of it as a test run; it may take you a little longer than everyone else, but who cares? My mum always used to tell me that "life isn't a race," which felt like hopelessly misguided advice when everyone else I knew was out there living their lives, but she was right. It took me far longer to complete education than anyone else I know, and I'm now living a life far better than the one I would have lived were I allowed to continue with unmanaged psychosis.

Prepare a roster of relaxation techniques

Lots of people are skeptical when you mention relaxation techniques, but relaxation does actually work. Whether you have clinical anxiety or not, exams can bring out unmitigated panic in even the calmest of people, so having a roster of relaxation techniques on hand when you're feeling particularly anxious can really help. There are breathing exercises, progressive muscle relaxation methods, and more at the back of the book.

Take time out

There is a tendency, during exam period, to feel as if every second not spent studying is a waste. This is not true.

Take regular breaks—hours if you need them, or days—to decompress and not think about reviewing. Break up your days by doing tiny acts of self-care—have a shower, or walk down the road to buy yourself something nice to eat. Splash some water on your face, take a day off, and lie in bed if you need to. Don't stretch yourself further than you have to, because therein lies the start of a depressive episode, of severe anxiety or maybe worse. Essentially: be kind to yourself.

These tips aren't the be-all and end-all. Obviously, even success also requires hard work and lots and lots of study. And it's not glamorous, either; "make some flashcards" may not be the insightful and revelatory mental health advice you were after. To say it "works" may be grandiose—but it certainly helps.

I eventually succeeded at university the third time round. I tried hard to stick to routines and stay on track and, while it was extraordinarily hard, I managed it. I didn't quite get the degree I wanted; I had always imagined myself leaving university with the highest degree, a tight-knit group of friends, and a raft of exciting, fun and pleasant memories. I managed none of this, but it didn't matter.

What I did manage to do was navigate depression and mania, recover from the worst psychotic episode of my life, and still get a good degree. The grades I received didn't, and still don't, matter in either an existential or a practical sense. I've never been asked about my degree since I graduated, but it represented a lot to me. Not to get too sentimental, but I've never been prouder than the day I sat my last exam. I had made it to the finish line, despite all else. It didn't matter how I had got there; it was circuitous and arduous, but I was in exactly the same place as everyone else.

I also realized how little it all mattered. I was pleased to have finished the course, obviously, but it was less because I now had a degree and more because I had proven something to myself. I had proven that despite everything—despite teenage depression and all the struggles I had experienced at university—my mental illness could never stop me from doing something I wanted to do.

CHAPTER 5

SELF-HARM AND SUICIDE

This chapter contains detailed discussion of self-harm and suicide. If you're likely to be affected negatively by these, please do take a break or skip the chapter. Websites and numbers of charities that deal with these issues are at the back of the book; if appropriate, please utilize them.

SELF-HARM

There are lots of good quotes about drinking. Hemingway and Bukowski and Kerouac have all provided alcoholics across the world with elegant barbs about their drinking habits. Drugs, too, have secured their place in the literary canon—in recent history, Burroughs and Huxley wrote paeans to the act of taking drugs, and in more distant memory, so did Byron and Coleridge. Each one of these writers lent an air of glamorous gravitas to addictive behaviors; legitimizing it, but also mythologizing it. The act of drinking or taking drugs, in the hands of these writers, was elevated from mere hedonism to something transcendental. Whether it was the experience of being drunk or high that made the act meaningful, or the subsequent battle of will, weaning themselves off their vice of choice, these men made addiction an art, and art out of addiction.

Self-harm (by which I mean cutting, burning, or other forms of self-mutilation) has not had any such literary sponsorship. Nowhere to be seen are the lyrical odes to self-mutilation; nobody, outside of Sylvia Plath, is associated with self-injury. The reason for this is twofold: one, the dominance of men in the literary canon; and two, the way we categorize the many forms of self-destructive behavior.

For what started in my bedroom at thirteen, as I limply and impotently pressed a pair of blunt scissors into my arm, extended far into my adulthood—into twenty-four-hour drug binges and sixty drinks a week, and total, exhilarating emotional recklessness. Self-harm is self-destruction writ large, after all. The only way it differs from drink or drugs is the physical mark it leaves on your body, the shameful evidence that you have a problem. It's less socially acceptable, but for many people it serves the same purpose: complete annihilation of the self.

Each vice is an elegantly designed shot, a vaccination against reality. When you're manic, drugs are an irresistible top-up to an already superb wave of powerful, arrogant joy. Alcohol kneads the rawest edges of depression into something softer and more manageable. For me, the greatest love affair of all has been my love affair with self-harm.

It sounds romantic, and in a way it has been. My relationship with self-harm was its own self-sustaining ecosystem. Secret out of necessity, my sole escape from the real world, it was almost like a real affair. Affairs are always found out, though; lies always unravel. And past the initial excitement, the rush of the forbidden, they're always unhealthy and always destructive.

There are lots of theories about self-harm, lots of reasons why someone might do it. There's the old "cry for help" theory, which dismissively posits that teenagers cut themselves purely for attention (as if feeling so desperately in need of attention that cutting yourself seems like the only option isn't a problem in and of itself).

Then a raft of other theories: the outward manifestation of an inner pain; addiction to the endorphins released by a cut; or a way of feeling something, no matter how painful, when you're otherwise numb. I'm still not sure what it was for me, what made self-harm so irrevocably enchanting. Some of it was the ritual: the glint of the blade, the thick hot blood, the scars that turned from red to purple to hard white lumps on the skin. And of course there was the pain element, too—the release of it, the little fucked-up masochistic thrill that accompanied every slash or burn or cut.

No person, relationship, or event even comes close to being as significant as my teenage self-harm was to me. It influenced everything. My first relationship, while just as meaningful and joyful and important as any other first love, was partly forged on a mutual appreciation for, or perhaps addiction to, physical pain—it was a secret we shared, a thing that set us apart in a vast sea of misunderstanding. My high school best friend was the same; our friendship was amazing, intense, but she too shared these masochistic tendencies with me.

I'm sure everybody at school must have known—sleeves that remained resolutely rolled down even on the hottest day, little glimpses of flushed skin, or not-so-mysterious white scars. I was also behaving oddly. As anyone with a secret can tell you, your ability to moderate your own behavior gets somewhat lost amongst attempts to cover your tracks.

You might be thinking that "addiction" is a rather grandiose term for self-harm. It's not. Self-harm is often written off as attention-seeking, and even more frequently as a "teenage girl thing."* What that means, in broad cultural terms, is that it is facile. It is self-serving, maybe, and it is narcissistic. Teenage girls aren't given much respect generally, so anything that's even vaguely related to them is treated dismissively. Girls generally have

* Research also suggests that self-harm is more likely to affect girls than boys, although this may be because boys engage in behavior that isn't classified as self-harm (such as punching walls). Nevertheless, the perception of self-harm is incredibly gendered—in a negative way. Andrea Barrocas et al., "Rates of Nonsuicidal Self-Injury in Youth: Age, Sex, and Behavioral Methods in a Community Sample," *Pediatrics* 130, no. 1 (July 2012): 39–45.

it worse, I think, but the lack of respect lasts for all of adolescence. You can't possibly know yourself as a teenager, adults say. You can't possibly experience anything real or sincere or profound. So what I experienced, and what many other teenagers experience, is written off.

So, what counts as an addiction? Broadly, it's a behavior you feel you have no control over that has negative effects on your life. I'm not sure how anyone else is defining it, because I can't see any better description of my self-harm than that.

For years, it was a compulsion. It wasn't a choice in any real sense—when I tried to give up, I couldn't. I relapsed time and time again—little marks on my calendar, counting cut-free days, turned straight back into little marks on my arms. I had help from parents, partners, friends, medical professionals; I blogged about it, tweeted about it, thought about it constantly. Still I couldn't give up. At my very worst, I was bringing blades and razors to school with me every day and sneaking off to the toilet during lessons and at lunch, getting a deep and illicit thrill from it.

I'm not alone in my experiences. A 2013 study of U.S. teenagers found that between 13 to 23 percent of teens had self-harmed, but it's hard to get a handle on the real figures.* The nature, and stigmatization, of self-harm means that many young people are unwilling to share details with friends or family, let alone with

* John Peterson et al., "Nonsuicidal Self Injury in Adolescents," *Psychiatry (Edgmont)* 5, no. 11 (November 2008): 20–26.

statisticians. Countless friends have had similar experiences—some who I had discussed self-harm with in the past, and others who only mentioned their self-harm after I started writing this book. There are thousands of young people across the country who have, or do, hurt themselves.

"It was a way of expressing how I felt on the inside," said one friend who described her experience with self-harm as "an absolute compulsion."

"I couldn't go a day without doing it," she told me. "It was all I thought about."

Another friend, a man, told me that it gave him "a sense of calm" that he just couldn't find anywhere else. He punched walls on a weekly basis—something many people may not even consider to be self-harm, though his compulsion was identical to mine, and the results pretty similar too.

All of the reasons I heard from friends were disparate—an outer manifestation of inner pain, a distraction from trauma, a way to channel anger—but one running thread was clear: "Nobody took me seriously." With the exception of one friend, who had supportive family, friends, and roommates, every person I spoke to had come across somebody who questioned their behavior or feelings. I heard it a lot, too: "Isn't self-harm just a phase? Don't you grow out of it?" It's tiring. Dealing with people who don't appreciate how desperate you feel, who think you're looking for attention, is just so tiring. Justifying yourself constantly, feeling as if you have to explain yourself—it's exhausting.

Then there's another section of the population: those who treat self-harm with unmitigated horror.

I never quite understood why everybody was so shocked by my self-harm. There are lots of ways that pain and self-destruction can manifest themselves—self-harm is just the most obvious. Drinking to absolute excess three or four times a week, as friends of mine have done (and still do) is not healthy. Being dependent on drugs or taking too many too often is not healthy. A compulsion to sleep around is not necessarily healthy—casual sex can be incredibly fun, but feeling like you need to have sex isn't good. What sets self-harm apart from these behaviors? I'm not saying any of these things are always inappropriate—it would be vastly hypocritical of me to judge in any way. I just find it puzzling that drink and drugs—which can be just as damaging as self-harming—aren't seen in the same way as physical harm of oneself.

I think the problem is the nature of self-harm, the tangible physical results of it. For many people, scars or cuts or burns are viscerally uncomfortable. They force people to acknowledge the reality of your pain; someone who drinks a lot or sleeps around, especially a woman, can be categorized under the conveniently neat term "mess." "Oh, she's a mess," people say, not taking into consideration exactly why somebody would behave like that. "He's having a hard time at the moment which is why he's drinking loads." It's all euphemistic, though. None of it serves to illustrate exactly how desperate a person can feel while they're careering from one bad hookup to another, one sticky-floored bar to the next. Self-harm is not euphemistic. It is blunt; it does not allude to anything. Self-harm says "I am hurting." It's an uncomfortable thing to hear, especially if you love someone.

It's a matter of relatability, too. Most people who drink or take drugs have gone too hard on occasion, or recognize the desire to do so. Lots of people have regretted a one-night stand. Self-harm, though, is an unknown quantity. It's out of most people's sphere of experience by quite some way. They can't relate, and that horrifies them.

Distraction techniques

It took me a long time to give up self-harm. I've pretty much kicked the habit now; I still do it from time to time, when I'm feeling really desperate, but the urge just isn't there in the same way it used to be. There's no compulsion now, no sitting daydreaming about knives or blood while I'm on the bus.

It wasn't easy, though. It took time, patience, and a lot of relapsing before I managed to wean myself off it. I had a daily battle with whether or not I even *wanted* to give up—it was my only emotional crutch, after all, and taking it away meant that I found it harder than ever to cope.

If you're thinking of giving up, though, there are a few things you can do to distract yourself. These are techniques that have helped me and various friends. They might not be a way of stopping entirely, but they can help give you a brief respite from the compulsive urge to hurt yourself. Even the Royal College of Psychiatrists has suggestions for distracting yourself, so there's a chance these techniques may help you out.

Coping techniques can be split into a few categories: **distracting yourself**, **comforting yourself**, **physical expression**, and **introspection**.

Distracting yourself

Distracting yourself is probably one of the easiest ways to delay or prevent yourself from self-harming—all you have to do is focus on something else (although, having said that, this is easier said than done). This could be:

- Watching a film
- Reading a book
- Doing a puzzle/crossword
- Playing a video game
- Calling a friend

Basically, this can be anything that will briefly distract you—whatever it is that you're into. I often find measuring this distraction out in strict time periods helps: "I'm not going to cut myself for ten minutes," for example. These small sections of time are easy to fill—one episode of a TV show is twenty minutes at least—and you may find that the desire to hurt yourself has passed or at the very least lessened in those ten minutes.

Comforting yourself

This tends to fall under the self-care category, so think of some of the techniques you learned in that chapter. Comforting things can be grounding, so they're most likely to work when your desire to self-harm is frantic and you need to calm down. Some ideas:

- Have a bath
- Have a nap—lots of blankets, lots of pillows, lovely soft PJ's
- Meditate or do some breathing exercises
- Smell something nice—aromatherapy oils can help here
- Put on some fresh pajamas and watch some TV

Physical expression

Physical expression is a good way of releasing pent-up energy *and* distracting yourself. There are some pretty corny ways of doing this—you're going to feel dumb screaming into a pillow, for example—but no matter how dumb they are, they can actually help. Ideas:

- Punch something (a pillow or a punching bag rather than a person, please)
- Squeeze ice between your fingers (this will also hurt because of the cold, so it can provide some of the masochistic relief you're after without any of the more severe and lasting damage of cutting or burning)
- Squeeze a stress ball
- Do some exercise—go for a run, walk, or cycle somewhere

Introspection

Introspection is less physically fulfilling than the rest of these suggestions, but it can both provide a brief distraction and also help you figure out what it is you're feeling or what the self-harm you're craving is compensating for.

- Write down your feelings—even if you delete them or throw them away, this can be a way of expressing how you feel without hurting yourself
- Talk to a friend about how you're feeling
- Express yourself creatively—write a poem or a song or an article

First aid and staying safe

I think distraction techniques are great, and I strongly encourage you to try them, but I'm two things: one, a realist; two, an ex-self-harmer.

I know firsthand how impossible it can feel to give up. I know the thrill you get from self-harming. I understand how great it sometimes feels in the moment of relapse. If you absolutely have your heart set on hurting yourself, then I absolutely cannot talk you out of it. What I can do, however, is make sure you're being safe.

After-care is important

If you burn yourself, then remove clothing from the area, apply lukewarm water, and cover with plastic wrap. If you cut yourself, first try to control the bleeding by applying pressure to the wound. If it's a large cut or wound, press the edges together. Clean the wound and cover it with a sterile dressing.

How to clean a wound

It may not seem it, but making sure that your cuts or burns are clean is extremely important. A very small cut I had once got infected, and it was not only painful but disgusting. It seeped and oozed pus, and it made my whole arm ache for days.

Cleaning a wound is actually very easy, and you don't need any special apparatus to do it—only things you can buy in any drugstore that you can easily store somewhere discreet if you don't want anyone to know. I have taken all this advice from the UK's official healthcare system guide to caring for cuts and grazes, and it has always served me incredibly well.*

Once the cut has stopped bleeding, clean it using regular tap water. Using antiseptic seems like a good idea, but it can actually damage the skin or cause your wound to heal a lot more slowly. Once it's washed, dry it with a (clean!) towel and apply a dressing. This can be an adhesive bandage or a dressing pad, depending on what's available to you. Change it regularly and keep it dry, and after a few days it should be well on its way to healing.

---

* "Cuts and Grazes," National Health Service, last modified January 21, 2016, http://www.nhs.uk/conditions/Cuts-and-grazes/Pages/Introduction.aspx.

Keep an eye out for infection

As I have said, infections are gross. They hurt, they're unsightly, and most of all they're dangerous. If a wound looks excessively swollen or red, or is suddenly hurting more than usual, then it may be infected. You may see pus coming out of the wound or feel generally ill. If you have any of these signs, please go to your doctor; the infection can be treated with antibiotics.

If you need it, get help

If you injure yourself too badly, **go to the emergency room**. Do not leave a serious wound unattended because you're nervous about what will happen if you go to the hospital.

If blood is pumping out of the wound in time with your heartbeat, then chances are you've hit an artery—please call an ambulance or get to the emergency room as soon as you can. Chemical burns should always, *always* be attended by a doctor.

You can find out more information on self-harm related injuries from the charities Self-Injury Foundation, To Write Love On Her Arms, and many more. There are also helplines and websites listed in the resources section of this book.

I don't self-harm as much these days, but that doesn't mean I don't harm myself in other ways; drinking, drugs, and other reckless behavior should also be considered self-harm. These things are far less frequent than they were, though, and the compulsion is far less overpowering. When I find myself thinking about cutting myself, for example, I don't feel the keen, sharp need that bubbled and broiled in my chest until I alleviated it with a razor blade or scalpel. My ruminations are now much more logical. *Maybe if I cut myself, I might feel better*, I think to myself very calmly. This means I do it much less frequently. If my emotions aren't strong enough, they can be fairly easily overcome by logic.

It's taken a combination of things for me to get to this point, though. I've been in therapy on and off for a long time, which has helped. I've come out and talked publicly about self-harm: anonymously at first, on a blog, and then more publicly as my career became writing for a living. Sharing stories with other people about self-harm—and making sure that it wasn't a secret anymore—was incredibly freeing for me. Some of its allure for me was the fact it was a clandestine thing, something I wasn't telling anyone. Getting rid of that stigma allowed me to deal with it properly: an adult relationship versus an affair.

Above all, the most important thing for me was taking it day by day. It ties in with SMART goals, and with the "take it ten minutes by ten minutes" technique; feeling as if I had to stop, with no time frame or strategies in place, was impossible. But by taking it day by day—and, within that day, hour by hour and minute by minute—I was able to slowly stop. A day is nothing; a day is easy. And slowly those days add up. Sometimes you have to start from zero again—that's nothing to be ashamed of. Slowly, steadily, one minute becomes one hour becomes one day becomes one year.

SUICIDE

Suicide sits rather awkwardly in the cultural imagination. Like addiction, it's somewhat romanticized; it's tragic and unknowable, it robs us of writers and artists and musicians. But it's stigmatized too, denounced; it was a crime across the world for many years, and the subsequent social, religious, and moral hang-ups associated with this legislation don't really seem to have dissipated yet.

Modern arguments against suicide may not take such an explicit stand against religious mores, but their basis is much the same; suicide is immoral because it goes against the "natural order of things." The sense of self that many of us identify with resembles dualism more than anything else. Most people unconsciously perceive their mind to be distinct from their body. Suicide is an attack on both of them.

Unlike most other phenomena that fall under the vague umbrella of "mental distress," suicide is not thought of sympathetically. Depression and bipolar disorder and anxiety are all stigmatized and stereotyped and misunderstood, but there's a level of understanding that even the most pigheaded are able to grasp. Everybody has experienced sadness or despair; depression is the most extreme logical conclusion of these things. Everybody's been nervous or worried about something—explain to a skeptic that anxiety feels like that but *all of the time,* and they broadly understand it. But like psychosis, suicide does not seem like the logical conclusion of anything. It's counterintuitive, unreasonable. It seems unjustifiable.

Suicide is what happens when you've had enough. It's what you contemplate when you're so backed into a corner that nothing else is an option. Nobody wakes up one day and thinks, *Oh, maybe I should kill myself*—it's not a decision that just happens without deep and extended thought.

I don't think there's any picking apart the morality of suicide; much better and more intelligent writers have done that before me, so there's not much point. But what I can probably do is talk about my own experiences of being suicidal—maybe to humanize it a bit, or maybe to make you feel less like you're weak or selfish or attention-seeking for even acknowledging that you might want to die.

A Brief History of Wanting to Die

The first time I really wanted to die, I was fifteen. As eagle-eyed readers will probably already have gathered, I was pretty depressed. I don't really know where the idea that I might kill myself came from, but once it materialized, it lodged in my brain, where it has remained ever since.

At first my desire to kill myself filled me with anxiety; it made me antsy, nervous. I think I felt as if I might find myself half-dead before I realized what I was doing. But as I got used to it—the planning, the deliberating, the endless tossing and turning of ideas and concepts and pros and cons—it became soothing in a way. It was after I realized actually *could* kill myself, I think; after I realized that suicide wasn't a philosophical concept or an uncontrollable human instinct, and started thinking of it in stark terms. My actual suicide attempts—which have been shoddy and ultimately (and obviously) unsuccessful—took me from the vague conceptual realms of "I wish I was dead" to a very real understanding that I could literally kill myself at any point. If I suddenly decided that life was ultimately a zero-sum game, that I'd achieved all I wanted to and there was nothing left in it for me, I could kill myself. It was actually quite calming.

Suicide is a curious kind of tunnel vision. When you're suicidal you think of nothing else: weeks lost to aimless daydreams that always end with you under the wheels of a bus or lying dead in scarlet bathwater. It almost becomes banal, like the doodles you do in a boring lecture or pointless meeting—if they were all incredibly detailed and involved coffins and organs and blood.

I often come across as glib when I'm talking about suicide, and I think it can be jarring for some people. It's not that I don't take it seriously—the opposite, in fact. I casually describe how I've planned so sincerely and comprehensively for my own death simply because discussing it in any other way is impossible for me. I just don't know how else to do it.

I think it's because it can be so surreal, so ridiculous, so counter-intuitive, to wish yourself dead. I swing between calm logic—"I was only doing what seemed to make the most sense at the time!"—and absolute disbelief, and can find no way to reconcile the two. I don't know how they fit together, really, how in the midst of experiencing profound despair I was able to conjure up the kind of systematic organizational skills I lack even when I'm stable. Every step of each suicide attempt was calmly and efficiently carried out with military precision. Normally, I can't even plan what I'm going to have for dinner each night of the week.

The despair of suicidality is much more visceral for me than the blank numbness of "normal" depression. Depression for me is numb and gray and lifeless; being suicidal is like the darkest black of the deepest void. It feels like something is constantly crawling across your body—and I mean that literally rather than figuratively. It's terror rising all the time without the climactic relief of a panic attack. It feels like someone constantly goading you to *just do something.* But any time you try to do something—anything—it feels impotent. Getting drunk does nothing to help; going out to see friends doesn't help. Self-harm doesn't help, and neither does sex. Everything feels as if it's leading up to some bursting, some breakthrough—instead, the pressure intensifies more and more. Despite the rhetoric, it doesn't feel like "giving up," because "giving up" is passive. It combines the nervous energy of mania with the misery of depression.

As I've said, though, it's also methodical and disciplined. It's browsing the internet to find out toxic doses of medications, comparing lists of drugs that have deadly interactions. It's waking up and planning your day in minuscule detail; get up, go to work—don't forget that leftover lasagna!—go to three different pharmacies at lunch to stockpile pills, come home, die. It's thinking ludicrous things like *I can't kill myself tonight because yesterday was trash day, and I don't want the garbage to rot and stink the apartment up, so I'll wait until next week* as if they're totally normal thoughts. There's this idea that anyone who thinks about suicide is "crazy" in the most pejorative sense, but for me, it just doesn't feel like that. For me, it feels like I'm making the most rational decision of all.

I think, at heart, that's what terrifies so many people about suicide. It's very easy to dismiss suicidal thoughts as somehow irrational, and in a way they are. We're genetically and biologically hardwired to survive, after all, and you could even go so far as to say that living long enough to reproduce is the most important purpose we have. Resisting that biological destiny is madness in the truest sense; it's absurd and mindless and pointless. To write off suicide as an expression of such senseless madness is the easiest explanation, because it says nothing profound or interesting about the mind, nothing worrying about the human existence. It demonstrates nothing but the human capacity for lunacy. It protects people from the worrying thought that such madness could touch them.

But most suicides aren't inherently about "madness"; nor are most people who think about suicide mad, whether they attempt it or not. Of course in many cases there's an element of "madness"—lots of people who attempt or think about suicide are severely mentally ill. But there's no getting away from the fact that at the heart of suicide is a deliberate and level-headed decision. At the point of suicide, people may not be able to understand that things will get better. But they're not swept away by hysteria. They're not delirious. They're just unhappy.

What to do if you feel suicidal

Talk to someone

The most important thing to do when you feel suicidal is to **talk to someone.** This could be your GP, another mental health professional like your therapist or support worker, or a friend. You can also call helplines like 1-800-273-TALK, which are manned by extremely well-trained and empathetic people, or if you're at university, the school's offered crisis hotlines.

There are also lots and lots of great resources online around suicidal thoughts. The nonprofit Samaritans has a website if you don't want to call them, and many charities have online support services.

You may feel too depressed to organize it, but going to see a therapist or counselor, if you don't already, can also be a really good step to take when you're feeling suicidal. This also goes for visiting your GP or psychiatrist to get medication or a referral to another team. If you feel like you don't have the energy to call and make an appointment, or to attend the appointment, try to talk to a friend or person you trust who can help you take the practical steps you need to go and speak to a professional.

Try to keep yourself practically safe and away from triggers

When I'm incredibly depressed and prone to feeling suicidal, the thing I am most likely to consider is taking an overdose. When I start feeling like this and am still in my right mind, I remove all of the medication from my home as far as I can. Sometimes I'll get a friend to stay with me, who keeps hold of any medication I need and gives it to me daily.

If you can, try to do the equivalent. Remove sharp objects from your house, or hand them over to a friend. One charity uses the example of someone who drives dangerously when suicidal—if this is the case with you, give your car keys to a friend.

It's not always easy to remove yourself from triggers or potential suicide methods, but these are small ways of insulating yourself from them until you feel safer.

Distract yourself

Again, this is a short-term solution—your best bet really is talking to a friend or professional about how you're feeling—but it can be a way of keeping yourself safe in the short term.

Distract yourself with the methods we discussed in the self-harm section; have a nice bath, watch your favorite TV shows, go for a walk, paint your nails—basically, anything to bide the time until you feel very marginally better.

Prepare in advance

Prepare an emergency plan, containing all of the above, for when you're feeling suicidal. Know in advance exactly who you want to contact and what you'll need to do. Have a box or drawer full of distraction techniques or self-care items.

MYTHS ABOUT SUICIDE

If you put aside the grander notions of suicide as romantic tragedy, you also find a number of even more troubling ideas. Peel back the layers of insincerity—"such a shame," "what an awful tragedy"—and you'll find many people's true opinion on suicide: that it's selfish, for example, or that it's an attempt at attention-seeking gone too far.

As mental health becomes a far more prominent topic, it seems odd that these myths should remain. Education remains vital here. When I spoke to a friend, Jonny, whose brother killed himself a few years ago, he told me that education might be "the key" to stopping myths. "I was taught about disease in biology, and physical fitness in PE, but we never discussed mental health to any degree." He thinks we should teach children about mental health—he describes schoolkids as a "captive audience"—and thinks the opportunity to "teach them right there and then about depression, anxiety, suicide, and mental health" is too good to pass up.

"In school you have the chance to let them know that it's not unusual to feel low. You have the perfect moment to try to end the stigma," Jonny said. "Everybody just needs better, more widespread, and more in-depth education on the matter of mental health, and to acknowledge that things aren't going to change overnight. It could take years, decades, or even generations to change opinions and beliefs, but if in the end it saves lives and keeps people around, it can only be a good thing."

Lack of education really does lead to the perpetuation of these myths—not only are they offensive, they're largely based on misunderstandings or flat-out mistruths. If you've missed the boat for a school-age education on suicide, here are a few brief debunkings.

MYTH:
Suicide is selfish

The thing you hear the most about suicide is that it's selfish. They "should have thought of their family" and things of that ilk are often thrown around in the aftermath of a suicide. It seems to suggest that suicidal people don't care about their friends or family, which couldn't be further from the truth. Wondering to yourself whether, or how, friends and family would cope with your death is a major part of suicidal rumination, and it's not a decision that's come to lightly. Nobody fails to consider these repercussions. Nobody.

In my opinion, nobody is ever selfish when it comes to suicide. The idea that someone has been "selfish" in their decision to commit suicide suggests that there were other options open to them: one where they remained alive but continued to suffer, or one in which their suffering came to an end. That just isn't how it works. To consider suicide, someone is at the absolute end of their tether. They can't possibly understand how they could carry on living. Selfishness doesn't factor into it, because selfishness suggests a surfeit of alternatives that just aren't available.

All of that aside, I think the main problem with saying that suicide is selfish is that it just isn't helpful. The stigmatization of suicide—and by extension, suicidal feelings—is still rife. It's taboo to talk about suicide; even now, with my extensive professional and personal experience talking about mental health, it's suicide that causes the most awkward winces or strained silence.

"Nobody told me to my face that my brother was being selfish, but it's certainly a feeling that's out there," Jonny told me. "You see a lot of memes that get shared on Facebook and Twitter about how we should treat mental health the same way we treat physical health, with a picture of a guy with a broken leg being told to quit crying about it or what have you. But there seems to come a point where people stop wanting to treat mental health the way they treat physical health, and that point is where suicide is involved."

He also notes that somebody could battle cancer for years, attend chemotherapy sessions, take their medication, but ultimately pass away. "Similarly," he told me, "someone can battle depression for years, go to therapy sessions, take their medication, but ultimately lose the battle too. In only one of those circumstances would the person who died be called 'selfish.'"

"It's a flippant comparison, I'll admit, but if people want to treat mental health as they do physical health, it needs to be followed through to its logical conclusion."

Demonizing people who have killed themselves is horrible for them, for their families, and for those who also feel like they might want to die. Your mum was right: if you have nothing nice to say, don't say anything at all.

MYTH:
People who are genuinely suicidal would never talk about it

This one doesn't actually seem like a myth on the surface—it's not as much of a value judgment as the rest of them, and it *kiiind* of makes sense. If you were serious, you wouldn't tell anyone, because that might obstruct you from completing it, right? Wrong.

In actual fact, research has found that many people who kill themselves have discussed their feelings or plans with others beforehand. The Samaritans also make the point that it's incredibly important to take a person seriously if they say they're suicidal. If someone confides in you about feeling suicidal, then don't think, *Meh, they won't do it.* Think, *How can I get this person the help that they need? How can I help them access the services that they might require? How can I listen to and respond to their needs?*

MYTH:
Suicide is attention-seeking

I kind of covered this with self-harm, but it holds true here, too. A very small percentage of people may use self-harm or suicide to "seek attention," but it's not a game. If someone has no way of expressing a desire for help or regard other than through harming themselves, then what they need *is* help.

In a stable state of mind, I would never *dream* of acting as if I wanted to kill myself for "attention," and that goes for the vast, vast majority of people who express suicidal thoughts. If they're asking for attention? Give it to them.

MYTH:
Suicide is weak

The idea that people who are mentally ill are "weak" is something that really bothers me. What does it even *mean?* That you can't cope with things? That you fail to complete tasks that "normal" people do? That you find things stressful? That you're deficient in some way? It's something that comes up with mental illness generally and suicide specifically, and it is *such bullshit.*

Waking up every day and feeling depressed is hard. Making your way through your working day as you go through psychological and physiological strain is hard. Dealing with traumatic experiences is hard. Ruining relationships and putting yourself at risk because you're manic is hard. Navigating the world when you're constantly anxious is hard. And you know what? Most people get through it. Most people work through their problems and reach a stage where they're living a fairly stable life alongside their mental health problems. They might relapse, sure, but people keep going. People have jobs and relationships and lives, even though they might be in intense distress. Does actually feeling this distress make them weak? Because to me, living every day with mental illness looks a lot like strength.

To suggest that someone is somehow weak because they decide that no, they can't deal with the immense pressure they're under, is abhorrent to me. It's judgmental; it says, "Well, *I* could probably get through it." It adds to the narrative that people with mental health problems are somehow not *trying* hard enough—if they just tried to be strong, they'd be able to get through it. Well, that just isn't the case.

When I've been my most suicidal, the idea that I have some kind of moral deficit—that because I can't cope, I'm broken and weak and too feeble to survive in an unforgiving world—has made me feel worse. It has made me want to die all the more. If I'm so inexorably weak, then what's the point? If I can't summon the "strength" to fight what feels like an unending battle, then my logic is right after all—I should be dead. This, of course, is not the case at all. If someone was struggling with anything else—mentally, physically, emotionally—you'd never call them weak: you'd ask how you could help. This, too, should be how you deal with suicide and suicidal thoughts.

How to Support a Suicidal Friend

So: myths busted, stigma ignored, what do you do next? What do you do if someone you love has expressed suicidal thoughts or you're worried about their behavior? As with all things, every situation is unique and context-dependent, but there are a few things to remember.

Withhold any and all value judgments

Most people are pretty good at avoiding this, but I have had quite a few experiences of confiding in people who respond to tearful, genuine pleas for help with "Don't be so stupid."

Of course, killing myself would be awful. But does hearing someone tell me I'm being stupid help? No. It does not. So even if you do have a less-than-sympathetic view of suicide, then please keep it to yourself.

Don't "bargain" with them

This is another one of those "I'm sure you probably mean well, but god, you're really not helping" things. Yes, I know I have plenty to live for. Yes, I know people love me. Yes, I understand in the vaguest and hypothetical sense that things can—and maybe will—get better. Telling me this doesn't actually help, though. Trying to bargain with me—"I'd miss you too much if you kill yourself"—doesn't help. I understand that everything involved in the statement is true, and well-meaning, and kind, but it doesn't help. It makes me feel guiltier, for one, and it makes me feel like even more of a fuckup. *How can I want to die with all of these people rooting for me? Why are they not enough for me? How did I become so self-absorbed, so selfish?*

Better, for me, is someone simply listening to me and acknowledging that my pain, and my desire to die, are valid. I'm not saying someone should tell me I'm *right*, as such—"Yeah, fair enough, knock yourself out"—but more that they appreciate that how I'm feeling is okay.

Even worse than this is, with all seriousness, saying, "If you kill yourself, I'll kill myself." There is no need for me to explain why this does not help.

Talk to them

Pretty much every chapter in this book has the same advice: talk to them!

Let's face it—talking about suicide is really difficult. But a few things you can do: ask open-ended questions which allow your friend to discuss as little or as much as they want; ask them how they're feeling about suicide to try to ascertain what their plans or feelings are; listen to what they have to say.

Encourage them to get help

Suicidal people are often resistant to seeking or receiving help, but it's still worthwhile to encourage them to get help. If they're worried about making appointments with doctors or psychiatrists, call for them or take them to their appointments. Help them find resources online. Even if these resources aren't particularly relevant, the fact that you've made the effort can often mean a lot.

During my last period of being suicidal, I had two particular friends who'd help me out: they encouraged me to go to the doctor; they took me to the pub once a week; we would have lunch all the time. They listened to me say the same things for weeks on end. They were patient and kind when I was rude or when I ignored their messages. This on its own was hugely helpful. The fact they encouraged me to get help was a bonus.

If you're feeling suicidal: I feel you. It's happened to me countless times, and I'm sure it will happen again, which gives me the authority to say: please get help. Talk to somebody, call a help line, tell a friend. Acknowledging that your feelings are valid and seeking help for them might feel scary or feel like a failure of some kind. It's not. It's brave, and it's vital.

I'm loath to wholeheartedly subscribe to the "it always gets better" narrative because I think it betrays a fundamental misunderstanding of how mental illness works, but so far I've managed more than eighteen months without trying—or really wanting—to kill myself, and I can't even begin to envisage myself wanting to die as much as I have done in the past. It seems faintly ridiculous to say I'm "proud of myself" for simply being alive—but when wanting to die is the norm, each day I'm still here is an achievement in itself.

If you need help dealing with suicidal thoughts, please check the back of the book for a list of helplines and resources designed to help you when you're suicidal.

CHAPTER 6

FAMILY AND FRIENDS

Families are complex and delicate ecosystems. The smallest thing can cause them to temporarily lose their balance; larger disruptions can change their structure and atmosphere forever. Each of these ecosystems is unique and impenetrable to outsiders, too, and navigating them can be an alchemic combination of experience, guesswork, and luck.

So what happens when this system is distorted by mental illness? How do families change when one of their party becomes depressed, or too anxious to cope? And how do you even communicate what you need from them?

The answer, rather unsurprisingly, depends on the family.

FAMILY

We all know how hard living with mental illness is (you're six chapters in, so if you're still on the fence, then I'm not sure I can help you) but what's often ignored is how it affects those around you. Of course, we all know people who make their partner's, friend's, or family member's mental health problem all about them, but in a more general sense there's very little discourse around the carers or cohabitants of those with mental health problems.

I've had mixed experiences in this area. My family is great, but it's not always been easy—particularly for my mum, with whom I lived more or less alone throughout my childhood, adolescence and, unluckily for her, adulthood.

The intersection between family life and mental illness is probably most evident during adolescence. Most people still live with their families when they're teenagers, and it's a time when mental health problems often start to develop. This makes things even harder: you're dealing with mental health problems for the first time, you're unsure of yourself to begin with, AND you have to get along with your family at the same time. It often makes for a rather unhappy combination.

I know my parents won't disagree with me if I say they initially dealt with my mental health problems relatively poorly. They've always, always *tried* to help; they've always tried to understand; they've nearly always acted in a way they felt was most appropriate. However, that doesn't mean they always got it right. My mum, confronted with my probably rather alarming self-harm habit, told me I was being "silly." Later attempts to bribe me out of self-harm via treats unsurprisingly failed, and I was often met with anger, exasperation, and disappointment when secret scars were inevitably discovered. Her reaction was altogether rational, though—of course she was angry, of course she was upset, of course she was exasperated. But it didn't go very far in terms of assuaging my guilt or undoing my destructive urges.

I felt as if she didn't understand because she just wasn't *trying* enough. Explaining the reasoning behind self-harm to yourself is hard enough in the first place, let alone trying to articulate it to your own mother. My arguments that self-harm was just the same as drinking a lot didn't go down well either; drinking was normal to her, and so, to an extent, were drugs. The fact that I would willingly cut myself was so far outside her frame of reference that she had no real way to process my secret habit. She dealt with it the only way she could—which is to say, she had no idea what she was doing. I don't blame her.

We also fought a lot when I moved back in after I dropped out of university. I had become used to exercising my own autonomy, and although that mainly consisted of sleeping in late and eating junk food at eleven o'clock at night, I resented having those spurious freedoms taken away from me.

I was also incredibly depressed. Having dropped out in a spectacularly ridiculous fashion, I had very few friends left from university, and I was forced to sit alone in my rural childhood home, literally and figuratively miles away from the schoolmates whose happy university experiences were documented in minute detail on Facebook feeds I bitterly obsessed over.

These factors conspired to make me even more miserable, as well as bitter and crabby and spiteful—basically, any synonym for "bad tempered." I rejected any attempt at affection, because accepting affection would require me to let my guard down, which was something I couldn't manage. My experience with psychosis had hardened me, and my subsequent depression wasn't doing much to soften my now completely glassy heart. As a result, I spent most of my time making barbed, and in hindsight not particularly funny, remarks about my family, what was on TV, people I saw on the street, a child who lived across the street who I had decided I hated, and most of all my own mother. I was a nightmare: this terrible, half-formed monster who had outgrown adolescence but failed to developed the critical faculties of adulthood. We fought in increasingly bitter ways.

I asked her about how she remembered the year, assuming she'd felt similarly. I was right. She described it to me as "one of the most difficult years of her life," something I'd probably agree with. Some of the words she described me with included "impatient, irrational, bad tempered" and "prone to complete meltdowns." I had panic attacks, which she was powerless to stop.

My mum's approach to dealing with a problem is talking about it endlessly, a habit partners will unhappily attest that I've inherited. Her desire to talk goes far further than mine, though. She thinks that talking is the secret key to everything. As someone who was deeply depressed, this approach irritated me. My mum, in her own words, "begged" me to go to the doctors, and though she still thinks my reluctance to go was irrational, to me it was understandable. I had been forced to drop out of university; I had no friends. I was thinking about applying to do another major, but a year felt like an impossibly long time, and there was no guarantee I would get in. What was there to talk about? More to the point, considering my circumstances, who *wouldn't* be depressed?

She was also incredibly keen that I go back to therapy, which I resented too. The days on which we drove to the doctor's office in palpably strained silence were the worst of all. I didn't want to talk, I just wanted to lie on the sofa and tweet inanities at strangers.

In the end, the therapy started to work. My job at a supermarket, though menial, gave me a new set of friends and a vague sense of purpose, and I slowly pulled myself out of depression. I was a lot easier to deal with then, I imagine, and was certainly a lot less acerbic. Still, the situation taught me a lot about living with someone who didn't really know how to deal with my mental health problems, and it taught me even more about how to talk to your family about mental health.

It's hard to talk about mental health with family members. It's really hard. I don't know why, exactly; your family are the closest thing to you, in both literal and figurative senses. While it's certainly not true in lots of cases, I think it's fair to say that most parents will love their children unconditionally, no matter what happens to them and especially if they have mental health problems, which are never anybody's fault. There's a tension, though, between remaining under the familial wing and being your own person—between asserting your bodily and psychological authority and yet, still, wanting reassurance and protection. It's a taut, tough tightrope to walk.

It can also be hard when more than one member of the family has a mental illness. My mum is incredibly anxious, and has experiences of severe anxiety disorders, agoraphobia, and OCD. If she's feeling particularly anxious, it manifests itself in obsessive checking—checking that light switches are off, unplugging electrical equipment, checking a very specific number of times whether or not the oven and gas burners are off. If I'm feeling stable, it's fine—I tell her she needs to get support, I try to help her out, I do the best I can. If I'm depressed, however, it can get ugly.

When we lived together, the depression/anxiety combination didn't really work for us. I was depressed; she became anxious about my depression. Her anxiety felt stifling to me and so I pushed her further away, became more introverted, made her more anxious. Her anxiety irritated me. Without the empathy I normally would have afforded her, it just seemed overbearing. We argued a lot and nothing was ever resolved. Only later, with the help of medication and hindsight, did I see what a difficult cycle we'd managed to get ourselves into.

My dad has depression, though as we've never lived together for any significant amount of time, we haven't interacted particularly explosively. His experiences of mental illness and parenthood haven't been as easy, though. His mum had many symptoms of what would now be diagnosed as bipolar. She was addicted, at various points, to prescription pills, cough medicine, and alcohol. This was back in the days when cough medicine had all sorts of junk in it—morphine and cocaine extract and other stuff you probably wouldn't get in a bottle of Robitussin.

She would send my dad, aged eight or nine, to pharmacists and clinics across their small Welsh town in the countryside, equipping him with excuses he'd recite in his head in the waiting room so as not to get them wrong. She'd lost her pills, or put them in the wash by accident, or lent them to a friend. It was fairly transparent, he says, and because they lived in a tiny town, everyone knew everyone and the jig was up pretty quickly. In cases like this, it can be even more difficult to deal with your own mental illness.

A lot of these difficulties come down to our old friend rumination. You identify yourself as a "mentally ill" person; you obsess over the disease's provenance; you find the finger pointing firmly at your own family. It's not necessarily even the case—although mental illness can be genetic, experts say that there's no real way of knowing where an illness comes from. Some conditions are more likely to be passed on than others—for example, the risk for bipolar disorder in the general population is around one percent, which is fairly small, but for those who have a first-degree relative with it, that number can shoot up to 10 percent. My grandmother was never formally diagnosed, but I've spoken at length to my dad about it, and there are a few pretty striking similarities between our behaviors. Likewise, my mum has never sought extended help for her anxiety or OCD, but there are certain behaviors and compulsions that are a fairly close mirror of each other.

It can lead to a level of resentment, if I'm honest. I've had moments where I blame my parents for my mental illness and wondered why they had me—not in an "UGH, I WISH I'D NEVER BEEN BORN," slamming-my-bedroom-door way, but in a genuine "you probably could have saved yourself a lot of hassle if you'd thought about it" way. I'm not judging them, obviously, and I'm certainly glad I'm here, but I have felt almost irritated by the fact of my own birth on more than one occasion. I've felt angry that they've seemingly passed on this horrible burden to me, as if mental illness isn't an accident of birth but some kind of Evil Stepmother curse they've purposefully decided to bestow upon me.

It's not like it doesn't go the other way too, though; my mum has expressed feelings of guilt about my childhood, worries that she'd either not done enough or had somehow "caused" my mental health problems. I worry, too, that it could happen when I have kids, and other than the fact that I'm supremely selfish, it's the one thing that really puts me off becoming a mother. It doesn't help that most of the people I've been with for significant periods have also been mentally ill to varying degrees too. Together, we could create some kind of horrible amalgam of mental illnesses.

The sense that something so horrible might be biological destiny was a feeling I struggled with for several years. I felt trapped, tethered to my family in a way that didn't feel altogether voluntary. They represented my inability to escape my mental illness. No matter what I tried, I would always have bipolar disorder, and I would always be tied to my family because of it. My genetics had betrayed me; so, subsequently, had my family.

At the end of the day, this kind of thinking is fruitless, both on a parent's part and on a child's. Did I inherit my grandmother's bipolar disorder, or my mother's anxiety? Maybe. But maybe not. It could have been an accident of birth. I could have been pushed to the edge of sanity by a particular event. It could have just been bad luck. Even if it was my genetic destiny to be mentally ill, there's no point blaming my family, as it's hardly something they've deliberately foisted upon me. **And, at the end of the day, no matter where my mental illness came from, only one person is responsible for managing it: me.**

How to live with your family without killing yourself or them

Beyond selfhood and rumination and all of the more conceptual, identity-bound stuff, there's something perhaps more pressing to deal with: the practicality of living with someone when you're mentally ill. Living in a family home is often different from more casual living arrangements like sharing a student house or living with friends, mainly because there's a whole different set of expectations.

I don't know about anybody else, but in my experience, the level of solitude I managed to uphold in shared houses was just not possible in a family home. Things like going out when you want, having people over, eating what and when you want—they all seem like fairly commonplace facts of life when you're an adult, but when you live in a family home, they're not always thought of in quite the same way. (If you're reading this and you've not left home yet, you have a lot to look forward to.)

It's a double-edged sword, really; having someone there to talk to during mealtimes or quietly watch TV with can be really comforting when you're feeling low or anxious. It can be nice simply to have the company, and also to have somebody who can curb your desire to hibernate alone.

It can also be incredibly annoying. Sometimes, I think, being alone is kind of vital. When you're depressed, you naturally withdraw, and you need time to recharge from social situations, which are exhausting and difficult. A family home does, of course, provide some level of solitude—it's not like you're being constantly forced to be cheery and outgoing—but your ability to be so solitary is definitely limited.

It can also be hard if you're not in a place where you can talk about how you're feeling. Maybe you don't want to tell your parents because you know they'd react badly, for example, or maybe you just don't have the energy or the words to talk about how down or anxious you're feeling. Living in such close quarters with somebody can make this hard. Keeping up a front socially can be manageable. Before I started writing about mental health so much, I had colleagues and acquaintances who would be genuinely surprised when I told them I had depressive periods. They never would have guessed, because smiling and laughing and having a drink is manageable for periods of several hours. It's surprisingly easy to pretend you're okay in the short term.

It's not sustainable all the time, though, and it absolutely does and will sneak out at home. Home is also where you're most comfortable, hopefully, and so you're quite often the most *you* when you're there; no pretenses.

So, as we can see, there are a fair few forces at work here, and they can often make for a weird mix: trying to stay sociable and bearable around your family, maybe trying to keep your difficulties from them a little, trying to carve out your own space for peace and quiet. For me, juggling these things has led to arguments, major fallings out, a horribly strained living environment, and increased anxiety. So here is my guide to avoiding those things, and living with your family as harmoniously as you possibly can.

Carve out your own little space

This goes for living with friends or on your own too, but carving out a little bit of peaceful, tranquil space can really help if you need to escape a fractious living situation. If you're still living at home with your parents, then you might have limited redecorating powers, but make your room as lovely as you can. Get a nice bedding set—you can get some pretty cheap ones now—or some string lights or some cool posters or some cushions for your bed. Get a bookcase and fill it with your favorite books. Basically, go wild with the decorating until it's a space where you feel comfortable, safe, and happy.

It might not seem like a big thing, but having somewhere you can escape to, a place that automatically makes you feel calmer, can really help you if you're having a bad time in terms of arguments, or if you feel like you want to get away from pretending to be okay and just relax. It was hard for me to get this kind of space as a teenager—my mum's anxieties meant I couldn't have things like candles or incense in case I burned down the house, and the furthest I really got with making my room my own was sticking some printed-out pictures onto my wall—but since I've left home, I really have started to appreciate the value of having a nice space that makes me feel secure. None of this has to be expensive, either—you can get string lights for about $5 online, $30 bedding sets at any place like Target, and rugs and picture frames for similar prices.

Assert your right to this space

Asserting the right to access this space without question is the hard part. Sometimes you can't just say, "Sorry, I need some space"; even as an adult, your motives can be questioned, your thoughts analyzed, your intentions taken as an insult. It can be hard to express that it isn't a slight on the people you need time away from, and that it's just for you. You can't always do it.

If you can, then great. Just say "I just need some time to chill out on my own," and go do your thing. If you can't, then lie: "I'm going to read my book" or "I have something to do for school/college/work and I need some quiet" or "I have a bit of a headache so I'm going to take an aspirin and hang out in my room." These are all totally reasonable excuses to go hang out alone, and are fairly likely to be unquestioned.

Obviously it's better if you have the kind of living arrangement in which your space and autonomy are respected, but it's not always that easy.

Communicate as best you can

Again, not always going to be useful advice, because communicating with your family can be awkward and difficult or, at worst, impossible. If you can, tell your family how you're feeling. Maybe they already know your diagnosis or know that you struggle; that's great. Talk to them about it as best you can, write them an email, whatever. Try, in whatever small way you can, to tell them how you're feeling or what help you need.

Develop house rules

This is SUCH boring advice. No nice "buy yourself some string lights" in this bullet point, let me tell you. It is, however, pretty useful, so listen up.

Set some house rules. Talk to your parents, siblings, housemates, whoever you live with, and try to establish some rules from both sides. Tell them you're happy to give and take (because compromise is basically the key to successful co-living) and concede points to them—you'll do the washing if they respect that you need at least an hour alone a day; you'll do some vacuuming in exchange for their letting you have your own space. If you can, try to clearly assert what it is that you want to get out of living together, and let them know that you're willing to both work hard and compromise in order to get it.

Plus, if things are clear and everybody knows where they stand, arguments over things like whose turn it is to wash up or do the laundry can be pretty much avoided. Cleaning schedules can help here; again, boring, unglamorous advice, but the little domestic strains that family life brings really can add up when you're already feelings unstable or ill. Avoid them!

The challenges of being a carer

Being mentally ill is hard; so is being a carer. Worrying about someone constantly, closely monitoring their moods even as you try desperately not to, picking them up when things go wrong. It's an underappreciated vocation, and it can be aggravating, irritating, frustrating, and rewarding in equal measure.

Having been on both sides of the coin in varying degrees, I feel like I have a fairly nuanced experience of the challenges of being a carer. Caring for my anxious mum didn't require excessive amounts of effort, and it was nothing like what some children go through when looking after mentally ill parents, but it was still unpredictably tough at times. Caring for various depressed partners has also proved to be difficult in ways I couldn't have anticipated beforehand, despite all my experience with mental illness.

The thing that nobody wants to say about mental illness is that it can often be really annoying. I know I'm annoying when

I'm depressed—canceling plans at the last minute, being hot and cold with friends and dates and family, alternating between needy and cold with alarming regularity. As I've said elsewhere, I'm also incredibly *irritable* at almost every stage of a cycle; depressed, I find the presence of other people incredibly difficult to bear; manic, I find myself resenting people for their slowness, their perceived lack of enthusiasm, their unwillingness to just keep up with me.

It must be unbearably difficult to love me. After I dropped out of university and moved back in with my mum, I spent a solid six months lying on the sofa. I'd get up, refuse to change out of my pajamas, lie on the sofa all day sleeping and looking at my phone, and then go to bed again. I didn't help around the house; I never once cooked her a meal or made her a cup of tea; I never did my own laundry; I only did the washing up under extreme duress. When manic, I've gone weeks or months without calling her or, alternatively, phoned her from the other side of the country to ramble on endlessly about some harebrained plan I had to make money or start a new course or relocate, and then promptly stopped replying to messages. It must have caused her unspeakable stress and worry. It must have been awful, and I can probably never apologize enough. And the worst thing is, of course, is the possibility that I'll do it all again. I'll never be "cured," because mental illness has no "cure," and so the cycle endlessly churns on with no end in sight.

When I spoke to her about it, the one thing she stressed was *patience.* It's incredibly important to have the patience and the foresight to know that the person you love, despite their problematic behavior or the fact that they might be pushing you away, is simply going through a hard time and needs your help. While they might seem like someone totally different—they might be snappier or meaner or just flatter and less outgoing—they're not. They're the same person you always loved, who you laughed with and had inside jokes with and had fun with. To nurse someone through an episode of poor mental health is to have the faith—and yes, again, the patience—to know that those things will happen again.

However, it's important to note that patience doesn't mean giving someone a free pass. If someone puts you down or argues with you over nothing or just straight-up insults you, you are under no obligation to just let it go. Illness can make someone difficult, but it doesn't excuse any and all behavior. So sternness can come in, too, or at least assertiveness.

There's an interesting debate here around autonomy and mental illness. At what point can you feasibly force somebody to do something they may not want to do but that's best for them? At what point, for example, do you absolutely insist that they go to a doctor about medication or therapy? When can you sit someone down and sternly tell them that yes, they are going to therapy this week, and no, you don't care if they don't want to go? When do you force someone to take a walk, or start eating better, or to get out of bed?

My mum has taken two routes: respecting my desires, even if they are counterintuitive and self-destructive; and forcing me to do things for what she saw as the greater good. Both approaches have had mixed results. Respecting what I wanted to do when what I wanted to do was lie in bed all day and eat four packets of cream buns was not particularly helpful. I had no reason to change my behavior. Because I'd dropped out, I had no responsibilities and, in my mind, no future. So why would I change? She hadn't put her foot down, I certainly didn't *want* to change, so what was in it for me? The nebulous, superficial concept of "happiness" just wasn't a strong enough motivator to get me out of my pajamas.

Then again, "I'm going to march you down to the doctor's office and get you seen RIGHT NOW" wasn't a particularly effective strategy either. I've found my mum's pushiness with matters of mental health rather overbearing at times. Being driven to therapy and being forced to go was probably good for me in the long run, but it drove a wedge between us for a while. I felt she was interfering with my life far more than she had any right to. She felt that I was irresponsible with my mental health, that my refusing help was immaturity rather than the pure terror it was actually borne from.

Of course, she was right to encourage me to go to therapy; I needed it. She was also right to tell me to get dressed, and to drink more water, and to leave the house every once in a while. She's probably right about a lot of the decisions I've made as a stable adult, things I've done when I've been medicated and therapized and happy. Unfortunately, though, as much as she might like to, she can't actually force me to do those things. It's not that she'd *want* to dictate what I'd do most of the time—in fact, she's always been very supportive of my often rather weird life choices—but that the line becomes impossibly blurred when it comes to illness.

How, as a carer, can you decide when the line is crossed between "letting someone get on with their perhaps very poor decisions" and "some incredibly dangerous decisions are being made here that need to be stopped"? The standard explanation—*when someone could cause serious harm to themselves or to others*—is impossibly reductive. As we know, there are plenty of ways you can cause serious harm to yourself that fall under the broad umbrella of "socially acceptable." A carer—parent, partner, sibling, or anybody else—can't stop you from making what they see as "bad decisions" such as going out and drinking late, or going on five dates in a week. The likelihood that someone is going to harm another person—which of course would warrant an intervention—is actually incredibly small. So what can you do?

Navigating the situation takes time, and is often a case of one step forward and two back. If you interfere too much? Step back. If you feel like you're being too passive, try to involve yourself—carefully!—with treatment plans or support structures. Now, my mum asks me what I need or what support she can give me and provides it. She gets anxious about me sometimes, of course, and it can sometimes veer into pushiness, but she's generally learned how to navigate my treatment and support.

Will you fuck up? Probably. Will it be okay, though? Almost certainly.

FRIENDS

In my experience, friendships are less complicated than family relationships. Or, at least, they're complicated in a different way. A relationship of some kind with your family is more or less inevitable; a relationship with a friend is opt-in. This gives it a different kind of closeness—you've chosen to be friends, after all, and so you have to be more gentle with it, more tentative. You can't treat friends as casually as you can a family, because they have no reason to stand by you other than loyalty or love. They can cut you off in a way families often never do—even if they should. It's no surprise, then, that I have lost a lot of friends. It's hard to tell where my difficult personality ends and my mental illness starts, but either way: I have lost a lot of friends.

Being weird is not easy. It's not easy for anyone, even the mentally healthy. Liking different things from everybody else—or being a different *kind* of person to everybody around you—is unspeakably lonely. Spending every day in the company of people you don't really like is a Herculean exercise in self-restraint. You feel as if nobody could ever possibly understand you, and in some cases you're right. You like the wrong things the wrong amount, you manage to say the worst possible thing you could say at any given moment. You find yourself spending most of your time thinking *Why the fuck did I just say that?* The friendships you do forge tend to be incredibly intense by necessity, which brings a whole new raft of issues onto the table.

So, as both a weird person and a person whose mental health problems make them even weirder, friendships have been a rather slapdash affair for me. I've gotten better at making friends as I've gotten older, though only marginally better at keeping them. And, predictably, most of the major fallouts I've had as an adult have been down to my mental health problems.

I understand they're hard to deal with. The intense friendships I form when I'm manic, and the level of sociability I'm able to maintain at that point, often fall to the wayside when I come back down to earth. If I'm depressed, I won't go out, I won't see anybody; I'll do nothing but the bare minimum. The last time my depression was that bad, I was lucky enough to have two friends (whom I've mentioned before and will mention endlessly to anybody who'll listen) who nursed me through it. I was pretty shitty to them, if I'm honest—at one point I deleted my Facebook, stopped texting them back, and ignored all calls—and they still persevered. Many others, perhaps rightly, have not.

There were my college friends, who we've already covered, who literally stepped over me as if our relationships were just a heavy-handed metaphor. My school friends, of whom there were very few. "But Emily," I hear you ask, "what about the friends you had the second time you went to college?" I can't say I had any bad experiences or problematic friendships there—but only because I had none. I kept to myself mostly, secreted myself away in a house I shared with an abusive boyfriend. Until I was about twenty-three, I had very few real friends. I had a few here and there, of course, several incredibly close friends, but I never had a "group," and none of them were at university with me. They were spread across the country in different cities. Like many things, a group of friends seemed out of reach to me. I was too weird to fit in anywhere, and slightly too insane to ever be part of the *Friends*-esque capers of my slightly abashed dreams.

For once, though, there's a happy end to this story. Unlike many areas of my life, which still require daily hard work, my social life has finally slotted into place. I put it down to two things: my best friend, and the group of friends I met when I moved to London after college. The latter are a group of intelligent, interesting, and creative people who are all either deeply empathetic or experienced with their own mental health struggles. I'm able to say, "Sorry, I can't come to the party because I've had a really bad panic attack" in the knowledge that they're not eye-rolling at me behind my back. I can tell them about my moods, and my past, and they're fine with it. They don't, as many people do, fetishize my mental illness; things I've done when manic, though often acknowledged as the great anecdotes they are, aren't treated like curios. To them, it's not a salacious insight into the weird world of a bipolar person, it's just a neutral value. It's just me. It may not be much to ask of a group of people—"don't ostracize me or act as if I'm a freak"—but it's rare to experience. Other people have had better experiences with groups of friends, I'm sure, but for me the simple act of having people around is still kind of special.

My best friend is essentially my soul mate. We share a taste in dark humor, and we have some of the same neuroses. She's funny, weird, dry, and smart in equal measure; she's as much of an attention seeker as me. She understands everything I express about my mental health problems immediately, even if they're bizarre or fucked up, even though she herself suffers from an entirely different set of problems than I do. She's willing to comfort me—but only up to a point—and is such a proponent of tough love that she's been responsible for innumerable successful interventions.

For people who are able to make friends normally, who aren't constantly worried about scaring people off with their mental health, having a best friend may not feel like such a big deal. So numerous partners have been abjectly baffled at the obsessive closeness of our relationship, of how intimate and romantic we are when our friendship has always been entirely platonic. I think it's because mental illness can wear you down to a point where you absolutely, wholeheartedly believe that something inherent within you is broken or wrong. Everything seems to confirm it; lack of friends, maybe, or social anxiety or relationships breaking down or failing to launch to begin with. And you become stoic about it.

So when you find someone who somehow *just fucking gets it,* who understands and empathizes and actually genuinely cares, it can make your friendship deeper and more intimate and more fulfilling than anything else in life. I'm certainly not one for sentimental transformation stories, where someone goes from deep depression to inspiring okay-ness because they met someone on the bus or they fell in love or whatever—I find them trite, mainly, and I don't think they address or understand on any kind of meaningful level what it means to be mentally ill. But for me, it's not hyperbole to say a friendship like this can save your life. It absolutely can.

Building a support network

Finding friendship like this is hard. It took me twenty-three years before I had a "group of friends" in any real way, because it was so hard to find and retain friends who are willing to stick around while I dealt with my problems. There are, however, a few things you can do to build this kind of network and also foster it healthily.

Be honest

There is absolutely no way you are going to maintain a successful friendship if you aren't honest. If you're not particularly close, it's fine—I'm not saying you have to share your mental health status with acquaintances or people you sometimes talk to in the kitchen at work. But in terms of close friendships, my policy is always that honesty is best. There's no separation between my mental illness and me; we come as a package.

The best kind of friendships tell you something honest and primal and essential about yourself. They let you be you in ways you couldn't explore or understand or discover on your own. In order to have that level of rewarding friendship, though, you need to give yourself up a bit—and that involves being wholeheartedly you, brain zaps and panic attacks and all.

Likewise, continuing to be that honest once you've achieved

this level of communication and understanding is also for the best. I've gone long periods without telling my best friend that I'm deeply depressed, and there was absolutely no point to it. I'm not even sure why I bothered; trying not to worry her, maybe, or hoping that if I didn't mention it then it would go away. Spoiler alert: it does not just go away. Telling your friends where you're at, even if it's hard to talk about, will likely help. At the very least, they can distract you with cat GIFs and links to articles and cups of coffee and maybe make you forget, for an hour at a time, that you're sad.

Get online

More on this later in the book. There are lots of communities online who can help you with your mental health—forums, specialist websites, Twitter. There are tons of people out there with similar conditions to you, people who just understand, people who will listen to you talk about how you feel and offer you genuine advice and help. The dynamic is different from a "real-life" friend in lots of ways—chatting with someone over email is different from having a cup of tea with someone, for example—but it's no less valid, especially if it helps you cope.

For me, having a big community on Twitter has been a saving grace on more than one occasion. Even when I've not actually been talking about mental health, there's always been a constant stream of pleasant conversation, shared articles, the minutiae of other people's lives. It's been a real comfort to me—and that's without mentioning the active support and advice I've had regarding mental health. It may not be for you—you may feel uncomfortable sharing your thoughts online, however banal—but it's worth trying out.

Get out and do stuff

There are two benefits to leaving the house and doing things. One: you will get closer to your friends, or maybe make new ones. Two: doing things is good for your mental health.

Not leaving the house is not healthy. It's understandable, sometimes unavoidable, but it's certainly not healthy. It exacerbates existing problems by failing to acknowledge them; it's stubbornly refusing to admit that the real world is anything other than an irritating subplot in the story that is your inner life. The more you stay inside, the harder it is to get back out there. For example, I've gone to parties or the pub after a few solid weeks of constantly staying in alone and I found my voice weak and small, my throat clogged with terror and indecision and my brain absolutely empty of things to say. Those interactions, it's safe to say, were not particularly successful. Instead of being fulfilling and fun social occasions, they actually strengthened my desire to stay in and see nobody, thus starting the cycle again.

If you join a club or go to the pub with some colleagues or meet up with your friend for a coffee, you will be doing a few things. You'll be opening yourself up to new experiences, for a start, which is always good. You'll be getting a small, low-pressure bit of social interaction, which is obviously great. And you'll be stimulated, physically and intellectually. You'll be getting fresh air, moving around. You won't be in bed, which is the most important thing. Plus, getting *back* into bed after a few hours out of the house is probably the single greatest thing a human can experience.

PRACTICAL WAYS TO HELP SOMEONE WITH DEPRESSION

Read lots of books about mental health and they'll tell you to *love* and *care* for your friends in the vaguest possible way. But when I need to help someone out, I'm not really interested in juggling *ideas* and *concepts*; I want cold, hard facts. I want lists of things I can do. I want to be genuinely useful. I actually want to help them. Do I want to instill a boyfriend with an ephemeral sense of joy via an inspirational meme? No. I want to help him get out of bed.

So rather than give you the kind of airy-fairy advice you might have received before, here is a (definitely not definitive) list of things you can do to practically help a friend who's feeling depressed.

Take them outside

As we've already covered, going out is good. Leaving the house is good. Fresh air is really good. Fresh air isn't going to cure someone of depression, obviously, but it can help temporarily lift their mood, make them feel more alert and awake and fresh.

They will probably not want to go. They will probably object to your suggestion that you leave the house. This is a time where being insistent can actually help, though, because you're encouraging someone to do a low-effort thing that has moderately high returns. Every time someone suggests I do this, I initially refuse, but when I'm eventually convinced into going, it really helps. I might be a whiny little baby about it while it's happening, of course, but I still do it, and once it's done I appreciate the effort.

In practice:

- Find somewhere peaceful, nice, or scenic to walk
- Make them a picnic and eat it outside (this may only work in the summer, or if you live somewhere that isn't constantly raining)
- Go for a cup of coffee or a drink—walk there and back
- Drive your friend somewhere quiet and fresh and undemanding like the beach, a river, a park, or somewhere else peaceful where you can wander

Do some chores

A really sucky thing about depression, amongst many other things, is its ability to render you completely incapable of completing normal tasks. When it's really bad, even showering seems like an impossible mission, let alone doing laundry or opening mail or cleaning your house. Helping someone do one, or several, of these things is probably the most practical thing you can do. It's also one of the easiest, because housework can be chopped up into loads of much smaller tasks that can be done as time is available. Having a tidy and clean house can really help someone's mood improve, too.

I recently went across the city to pick up a prescription for a friend who couldn't manage it himself. It took maybe an hour and a half out of my day and a minimal amount of energy. I sat on the train for an hour, I walked to the pharmacy, I talked to the pharmacist, and I left. No big deal for me. But for my friend, it was. Not only had I managed to do something practical for him, something that had desperately needed to be done, but I'd also shown that I cared enough to make that effort—which, briefly, made him feel a little less miserable.

In practice:

- Make an avoided phone call on their behalf. This could be to make a doctor's appointment or to call a plumber or something—something small that they've been putting off.
- Go through their unopened mail with them and sort them into piles—things to do, things to file away, things to throw away. Help them shred unwanted letters.
- Do some laundry for them—if you wanted, you could combine the walking idea and wander down to a laundromat with them, or you could simply go round to their apartment and shove a load in the washing machine.
- Do some dishwashing or other cleaning. This is something

I struggle with even when I'm not depressed—keeping up with the dirty dishes. Having someone come in and help me with it can make a big difference.

- Take out their trash.
- Help them with admin stuff: taxes, bills, doctor's appointments. Even if you just sit with them while they do things themselves, rather than actually taking over, you can offer some vital support.

Food, food, food

A healthy relationship with food can be one of the first things to go when you're having a crisis. You either eat nothing out of lethargy, or you binge on chips at 2:00 a.m. Hot meals? What the hell is a hot meal? Five a day? LOL nope.

In practice:

- Take your friend out for dinner—doesn't have to be super expensive, but dragging them out of the house and making them eat some delicious and healthy food can make a big impact on mood.
- Invite them round for a meal. Make everything cozy and warm and nice—make them feel at home.
- Order takeout, either remotely or to share with them.
- Do some grocery shopping for them and cook with them.
- Bake them some healthy treats.

There are even food delivery services now, which select healthy meals and send you a weekly box with ingredients and recipes in them. Your friend might not be up for cooking every day, but if they are, then this can be a way to show you care AND make sure they're eating enough vegetables.

Make them a care package

This is obviously super-personalized, so the list below is just a really vague example. But this can be a helpful and thoughtful way of showing you care, especially useful if your friend is in hibernation mode and doesn't want to go out.

A friend of mine, who is severely depressed, gets a care package from a friend every month. He packs it full of books and sweets and little Post-it notes with in-jokes and cute messages written on them. The days she receives them are lovely; she's always so pleased and proud and comforted by the fact that someone repeatedly takes the time and effort to send her things to make her feel good. It doesn't have to be this frequent, of course, but the fact that her mood lifts so obviously and dramatically, even for a little while, makes me a firm evangelist of the care package.

In practice:

- Something that tastes good—nice tea bags, something you've baked

- Something that smells good—candles, incense, perfume, bath salts, body lotion
- Something that feels good—a blanket, some fluffy socks, new pajamas
- Something to occupy their mind—book of crosswords, word searches, or Sudoku (these are my nerdiest and best coping strategies), a magazine or book of comics (basically something untaxing and simple)

This can be particularly good when you're really close to someone because it can be so easily personalized. It's not just about the items, of course—it's a statement that you care about someone, that you want them to look after themselves, that you know them, that you're just *there*. If you haven't got the time to put a whole box together, you can always order your friend something online too.

Listen

This is super easy. So easy, in fact, there are only four steps.

1. Shut up
2. Listen
3. Ask your friend what they want or need from you
4. Do that thing

This isn't an exhaustive list of ways to help, of course, and it's important to remember that no matter what you do, you're not going to make your friends not-depressed. These are just a few practical ways in which you can make your friends feel loved, attended to, maybe temporarily relieved of stress and depression.

CHAPTER 7

THE INTERNET

It's hard to think of one aspect of my life that isn't inextricably linked to the internet. I've met several serious partners on the internet, and most of my friends. I got a career in writing from the internet, a job, a book. I learned how to be myself online; I became a feminist because of online discourse, I read reams of badly scanned PDF versions of essays and books and papers that have shaped the way I think about myself and the world. My self-image, the conception I have of my own body, the way I inhabit myself, are all linked to my presentation online.

It is no surprise, then, that there is a complex relationship between my mental health and the internet. It's acted variously as a trigger, an emotional crutch, a lifeline, an addiction, a distraction. It's exacerbated problems that already exist and probably created new ones, but it's also been a vital source of comfort, knowledge, insight, and understanding. I just can't overstate what a significant impact it's had on my life.

Like most people my age, I first started using the internet when I was about twelve. I would go on a few AOL chat rooms, play Neopets, all the standard early 2000s stuff that anyone younger than me would probably see as some kind of terrifyingly ancient relic. And they'd be right—the internet speeds truly were horrifying.

Then, one summer when I was about fourteen, my mum started working incredibly long hours and I was forced to spend long days alone during the holidays. None of my school friends lived near me; those who did I was mainly focused on avoiding. So instead of reading or writing or doing something productive, instead of leaving the house or seeing friends, I did what any self-respecting introvert would do: I went online.

It started in small spurts—I'd go online for a few hours before wandering back to the living room to flick through books or watch TV. This was before the days of affordable laptops, of course, so I was confined to one tiny room to use an unwieldy desktop device. At first, I found the room claustrophobic. My family referred to the room as "the study," which to me conjures images of a big desk and a tidy pen holder and some nice paintings on the wall. In reality, it was little more than a cupboard, with the bookshelves that lined the walls making the room even smaller and more oppressive. The piles of books on the way to the computer chair added to this cramped and cloistered atmosphere.

Then I started going for longer bursts—five or six hours at a time. By the end of the holidays, I was getting up at 8:00 a.m. to log onto my slow-running desktop, only logging off when I had to go to bed at 10:00 p.m. I started getting up in the night to go online, sneaking past my mum's bedroom, careful not to wake her, to sit in the blue glow of a screen. When she started getting suspicious about my nocturnal activity, she'd check to see how hot the top of the computer tower was, so I started wrapping ice in a towel and placing it carefully atop the tower so it wouldn't get warm.

The most obvious reason I found so much solace online comes down, yet again, to my innate weirdness. Though my tastes tended toward the obscure compared to what went on in my tiny suburban village, they're certainly on the tame end of the scale when it comes to the internet, and it was easy to find people who shared my interests and philosophies. Feminism and left-wing politics were frowned upon by my peers, most of whom were conservatives, but on forums and chat rooms I found people who shared my point of view. My obsessive enthusiasm about the things that I loved was normally mocked, but online it was genuinely encouraged. There were thousands of tiny silos of people, all of whom loved the same things as me to the same degree, all of whom understood what it was like to be strange and alienated and lost in the world.

It still amazes me now, scrolling through my Twitter feed and hanging out with my internet-sourced friends, that there are so many people who get me and share the nichest of niche interests with me. When I first gained access to this world, it was genuinely mind-blowing. It genuinely felt radical and exciting and important—because it was.

Because I had this space, which felt so uniquely my own, I

tentatively started thinking and talking and writing about how I was feeling. The way I expressed these things wasn't great, I have to admit—as I've already said, I was into Morrissey and Sylvia Plath, and I romanticized my misery because I had no other way of conceptualizing it. I mainly wrote bad poetry that I posted on MySpace. I got lots of compliments on it, though—weirdly—all from the many older men who attempted to populate my Top 8.

To have people tell me—and perhaps more spuriously, to have numerous internet quizzes tell me—that I might be mentally ill, rather than just sad or bored or a teenager, was one of the first times I felt as if my experiences were valid and worthwhile. To hear other people say, "Oh yeah, I have that too. I feel those things too," gave me the confidence and strength to push forward in seeking help, and in feeling like I wasn't just some awful attention-seeking brat.

As I've become older and more self-aware, the internet has played less of a role in my self-discovery and more of a role in self-care. I use my main Twitter account for promoting my writing and telling dumb jokes about my cat. But I have a second, locked account where I tell a select group of people about my problems, where I discuss my day and look into their worlds and feel a sense of deep comfort. It's a tiny community that harks back to the early days of the internet; oversharing, tweets about the minutiae of someone's day, tweets about their dinner or their boyfriends or their jobs. This constant stream of banality has gotten me through so many bad days. Most of the people I talk to online in this context have experience of mental illness too, so a few rapid-fire tweets about a panic attack, or an urge to self-harm, are quickly met with genuine understanding, reassurance, and practical advice. During a particularly bad panic attack, several people distracted me by talking to me about their days, and one sent me a breathing exercise via a GIF. It helped a lot.

I think just knowing that there are people a few clicks away who really understand mental illness and are willing, at any time of day, to talk to me about it, is the most reassuring thing of all. Mostly, I use my private Twitter account to talk about how I just had a totally delicious orange juice or masturbated or my bank account is overdrawn, but it's a tiny oasis of calm and support in an otherwise chaotic life.

That's not to say that the internet is wholly a force for good. My obsessive checking of MySpace as a teenager, or twelve-hour stints online, were not and are still not healthy. Shutting myself inside and doing nothing but watching Netflix and sending tweets into the void is not healthy. It's very easy to get obsessed with the internet when you're depressed in particular, because it's so accessible, so perfectly designed for introversion and escapism. If I don't want to, I don't have to speak to a real-life person for days.

When I first started out as a freelance writer, I worked from home, and I would go days and days without seeing another human being. The most face-to-face contact I got was saying "thanks" to the guy who brought my online shopping to my door. Occasionally I would venture to the corner shop to buy some cigarettes and talk to the guy who runs the shop. It wasn't healthy behavior. I was steadfastly attempting to avoid reality, and having contact with either real-life or online-only friends, pretty much twenty-four hours a day, facilitated that.

This, as my ice-packed desktop tower could tell you, can be a problem. It's very, very easy to get addicted to the internet, which is a problem in itself. A 2014 paper suggested that young people and teenagers who spend too much time online are "at risk of developing anxiety and depression," and while, with my lack of medical expertise, I'd be loath to ascribe any particular factor to the development of a mental illness, I can say that in my own experience, it has definitely served to exacerbate my problems.*

HOW TO STAY SAFE ONLINE

One of the major problems I've had online is the huge abundance of pro-self-harm and pro-suicide communities. These have come under far more scrutiny in recent years, with several cases of people being encouraged to kill themselves by faceless internet strangers. This is unlikely to happen to you; the number of people who want to help, or at least to listen, far outweighs the number of people who want to push you toward suicide. Worrying as these cases are, they're an anomaly. The real problem is that the sites exist at all.

---

* S. Bahrainian et al., "Relationship of Internet Addiction with Self-Esteem and Depression in University Students," *Journal of Preventive Medicine and Hygiene* 55, no. 3 (September 2014): 86–89.

Browse Tumblr or Twitter, or just Google a few vague phrases, and you'll come across blogs and forums dedicated to self-harm, as well as thousands more dedicated to eating disorders. These are more often than not harmless; they're support communities, designed to help people out. But there are also websites that tell you how to cut and where, which foods to avoid and how to hide uneaten meals, even which combination of pills will most effectively and painfully kill you. It was these sites that pushed me further and further toward suicide, that helped me formulate plans, that made me feel as if my deep, despairing depression was a reasonable lifestyle choice. It seems superfluous for me to even have to say "don't visit these sites," but seriously: **do not visit these sites.**

Install a website blocker

In an ideal world, it would be great to say "just turn your computer off" when you're feeling tempted to visit pro-self-harm or pro-suicide websites. Unfortunately, we do not live in an ideal world, and to give you that advice would be incredibly impractical of me.

Instead, install a website blocker. There are about a million different options—browser plug-ins or programs you download to your computer—some stricter than others. Some will block certain websites for a small amount of time—twenty minutes or half an hour—but some are incredibly strict, and even if you turn your computer off or on again you can't access the sites until the time is up. Lots of these apps also make it impossible for you to uninstall them while a block is on, which means you pretty much have no way around it.

It's not a perfect solution, of course, and you may not have the willpower to always click the button to block the sites, but if you can feel yourself nearing the terrible tunnel-vision phase of an episode, these can really help. They're also a great tool for improving productivity when you're feeling down, distracted, and unable to concentrate, so are worth looking into for more than one reason.

Change your privacy settings

Sometimes, posting about how bad you're feeling seems like the only thing you could possibly do. You want to express yourself; you want to share your pain. I often find myself typing and deleting cry-for-help tweets over and over again, or feeling this odd and implacable urge to just *say something* to express how I feel. But in a public setting, like a public Twitter account or Facebook page, it is rarely a good idea.

This is not advice I give without vast prior experience. I'm better at it now, but for the past ten years I have been absolutely terrible about posting miserable things when depressed; mostly vague, mostly useless. I've also been guilty of posting frequently, and embarrassingly, when I've been manic. It's worst when I'm psychotic, but just being slightly high is bad enough in itself, because I'm prone to posting maybe a hundred tweets a day. Afterward, I generally feel embarrassed, and I mostly delete the posts.

When I look back at most of these posts, especially on

Facebook, the comments are mainly populated by people who, in hindsight, I know didn't really care about how I was. They were interested because I was being vague and odd, because they were nosy and they wanted gossip, because they wanted to barge in and feel important. If any of these people had cared, I feel as if they would have contacted me privately, which they rarely did, or would have done something more practical. They would have asked me if I needed help, or they would have contacted a member of my family or a close friend to check up on me. They never did.

Another imperfect solution to this problem lies in privacy settings. Facebook has settings that allow you to specifically tailor an audience for each of your posts. You can share something publicly or with your friends, or choose specific people to hide your posts from. When I feel as if I'm getting depressed or manic, or am aware that I'm having a particularly bad episode, I change the default audience setting to "Only Me." If I want people to see the post, I have to manually change it, giving me a small pause to think about what I'm saying, who I'm choosing to share it with, and whether or not it needs to go out to more than six hundred people, many of whom I don't even really know. It very rarely does.

This is a lot harder if you use Twitter because there are pretty much only two options: locked or public. Locking your account doesn't prevent people who already follow you from seeing your posts. At times when I feel really awful, I deactivate my Twitter account to stop myself from compulsively tweeting. You can deactivate for thirty days before your account, followers, and tweets are deleted permanently, which is plenty of time to consider how you feel and hopefully move away from a desire to compulsively post.

Keep an eye on how you're using the internet

Try to be aware of how much you're using the internet and what you're doing once you're online. Are you using it in moderation, or are you sitting up until 4:00 a.m. and going to work or school bleary-eyed and exhausted? Are you chatting with friends, blogging, and reading interesting things, or are you visiting websites about self-harm and suicide? Are your posts generally positive or neutral in tone, or are you finding yourself increasingly posting negative, pessimistic things?

If you keep an eye on the way you're using the internet, it can really help you monitor both your moods and the problematic behavior that may be associated with your internet use. This is where mood diaries can come in handy again. Adapting a mood diary to log your internet use can be incredibly useful. What time are you using the internet? Do you log on or post when you're feeling a particular way? What are your thoughts when you're using the internet? Writing these things down, or at least asking yourself the questions, can be a good way of discerning which behaviors are problematic and which are not.

Don't use the internet as a replacement for a therapist or doctor

Finding out information about your diagnosis online is good. Researching conditions before you get a diagnosis can be good.

But it's important to remember that the internet is absolutely not a replacement for a doctor.

It's easy to find online tests that tell you whether or not you have a particular disorder. In one afternoon you can diagnose yourself with every personality disorder under the sun (and trust me, I have done this). But these tests, even if they are the same tests administered by a doctor, are not a replacement for actually seeing a doctor. In a lot of cases, they're not even medically sound and have absolutely no clinical basis. There is no way you can accurately diagnose yourself with them, even if they do give you a vague idea of what you might be going through.

They're an okay starting point if you're at the beginning of your mental health journey and you're trying to work out what you're experiencing. But you really do need to take them with a pinch of salt. Consider them as an additional tool in an arsenal that also includes mental healthcare professionals.

Set aside phone- or computer-free time

Being online is great. The internet is great. But—and bear with me on this one—so is...not...being...online. I know, I know, it sounds fake. But it can be genuinely helpful.

Try to keep a healthy balance between time spent online and time spent offline. It's harder than ever to draw the line between the two—time spent hanging out with friends in person is often punctuated by tiny spurts of cellular internet use. But if you're online more than you're offline, and time spent with your friends or family is invariably accompanied by the constant presence of your phone, then it may be time to have a break.

You don't have to quit the internet altogether, but it may be worth setting aside some time every day without a phone or computer. Before bed can be a good time for this, as research has shown that looking at a screen before you go to sleep can affect sleep patterns and quality. Start slowly—ten-minute breaks from the internet at first, before slowly building up to longer periods offline.

Temporarily deleting accounts can help here, as I said above—breaks from Twitter and Facebook at the peaks of episodes have been invaluable for me, as they've given me time and space to think about myself and my feelings, and to alter my behavior. Breaks from the internet also force me to go and speak to people and leave the house and do all the kinds of things that normal, sane people do—and while I'm never going to be one of them, it can be nice to pretend for a bit.

HOW TO MAKE SURE THE INFORMATION YOU'RE GETTING IS CORRECT

One of the other major benefits of the internet is that it makes large amounts of information available, mostly for free, to anyone. Outside of the opinion-based worlds of social media and blogging, it provides endless facts too. Textbooks, novels, academic papers, encyclopedia entries... There's not much you can't find online. It can be a great resource for learning more about your mental illness, informing your opinion and understanding of things like medication, therapy, and just the basic psychological and biological details of your own illness.

Unfortunately, the internet also has an awful lot of crap on it. The fact that anyone can post anything they want online can be a good thing—marginalized people are given a voice and a platform previously denied to them, which is revolutionary and radical and wonderful. But it also means that people who have no real idea what they're talking about with regards to particular topics are able to write whatever they damn please about those topics. I've had lots of interesting and empowering debates online about different aspects of mental health, but I've also seen people say potentially dangerous things, misinterpret and then disseminate incorrect ideas, and sometimes straight up lie. So what do you do when you're looking for information online and you don't know what to believe?

Visit websites you trust

Check out the resources section of this book to find a list of mental health sites. All of these sites give you verified facts about mental health in a clear, concise and, most importantly, trustworthy way, and are also staffed by knowledgeable, approachable teams who, should you need to get in touch, are happy to provide you with more information or clarification on particular topics. All of these sites have a social media presence, too, so you can get in touch with them there if you're not up for using the phone.

Double-, triple-, quadruple-check

The information you're reading might seem correct, but before actually acting on any advice, it's best to double check that it's based in fact. First: Google it. Has anyone else on the whole internet said it? If so, who? Was it someone reputable and trustworthy, or are there just a few badly written blogs?

If you're still not sure, contact a charity or mental health professional, especially if the advice has the potential to cause more harm than good.

Don't be afraid to take it offline

It's nice to have the internet to help you with even the smallest of questions, and it can be especially empowering if you're nervous about talking about your mental health problems out loud or in real life. But don't be scared to take your worries offline.

A GP, counselor, psychiatrist, or psychologist is, on balance, better equipped to deal with your questions than a stranger on the internet. Sometimes their treatment isn't perfect; nobody's denying that. But they are trained and experienced and have qualifications that allow them to give you the advice and help that you need.

I've still not really shaken my obsession with the internet. When I'm depressed, or manic, my online life is one of the first things to be affected. I post too much or go off the grid for too long; I ramble and obsess and stay up until 6:00 a.m. looking at stupid memes or totally exhausting Netflix's supply of serial killer documentaries.

But what I have done in more recent years is take a mindful approach to how I use the internet. This can be hard and has certainly been challenging for me because of how ubiquitous the internet is now. I'm an online journalist, so my work is online. I research articles online. I am an embarrassingly prolific Twitter user. My friends use the internet in the same way I do, so we organize events and nights out and trips to the pub online. It is part of my life in such a way that I barely think about it anymore; cyberspace is no longer the separate "space" it was ten or fifteen years ago—rather, an extension of the tangible physical reality that I exist in every day.

But as with anything else, moderation is key. Drinking is also a part of most people's lives. They'll have a glass of wine with dinner, or a beer after a shitty day, or they'll meet their friends in the pub. That doesn't mean their behaviors around drinking aren't moderated, though—they certainly are. Most of us know when we're drinking too much, or if we've binged when we shouldn't have, or if we're spending more hours of the day drinking or thinking about drinking than not. internet use should be no different. Careful, mindful behavior that takes into consideration usage and mood may seem like unusual behavior—but in an age where the line between "real life" and "the internet" is increasingly blurred and often arbitrary, it's a vital tool for good mental health.

CHAPTER 8

RECOVERY AND RELAPSE

When I'd finally recovered from my first proper breakdown, I thought I had things figured out. I had been psychotic, yes, but I thought it was a matter of circumstance; I had a little depression, sure, but I wasn't *mentally ill*. I'd recover from it fully, I'd get back into the swing of things and go back to university and live a normal life again. I'd avoid the triggers that caused me to break down to begin with, get some sleep, and not drink too much. I'd dutifully take my medication every day until I no longer needed to—maybe even forever. I just didn't think of mental illness as a chronic condition. Essentially, I was positive.

This attitude was strengthened when I got into a "normal" relationship with a "normal" person. The fact he turned out to be abusive and controlling wasn't the point; we did normal-people things, like going for overpriced breakfast in cafés with exposed brick walls and saving up for a mortgage on a house. We looked at engagement rings and discussed baby names. We did things, in short, that I had no particular interest in, but that I felt were necessary parts of leading a "normal" life. I thought these things would protect me, as though a cheap vintage engagement ring would be a talisman that could ward off breakdowns forever.

I was wrong, of course. And the fact that I had bought so heavily into the lie made it harder to deal with when it eventually and inevitably went wrong again. Recovery was supposed to be a straight line, I thought. I was supposed to start at the very bottom, nestled between the *x*- and *y*-axes, and slowly move up and away from it. I was supposed to keep rising—no sudden dips back down toward zero. So when I did, it was crushing.

Mental illness isn't as cut-and-dried as some people would have you believe. There's no "ill" and "not ill." There's no "well" or "recovered." It's a sliding scale, a spectrum that we all move up and down no matter how sane we might be. Studies show that diagnoses are more complicated than we thought. The diagnostic criteria of certain illnesses may seem black and white, but they're not. It's rarely as simple as my being "well" or "ill"; I'm always somewhere on a scale of one to ten. It might seem odd to qualify mental illness like this—I'm six mad today, but I was eight mad yesterday—but it's a nuanced and complex and nebulous thing that just does not fit into a binary. The same goes for recovery.

At first, I didn't know this. I thought recovery was easy. Even the word "recovery" belies the tangible reality of living day to day with a retreating mental illness. But when is a person "well"? What does "well" even mean? Lots of government-endorsed studies say "well" is when you can function at work, which seems an unsatisfactory marker to me. Not only is that bound up in all sorts of cultural expectations about what makes a person productive and useful, but it also rings untrue for me; I've diligently shown up to work every day during the very worst episodes of mental illness I've ever had. By those standards, I was well. I was able to hold down a job, just. But I was emphatically *not* "well"—during that time, six of the eight hours at work were spent pondering suicide, drinking until I was sick every night, and self-harming badly, too. I wasn't well at all.

What about when I'm not suicidal, though? Day to day, I'm still affected by mental illness. As I write, I've been medication-free for a year and, aside from a few admittedly major blips, have been fairly stable and steady. I self-harm rarely. I drink far less now, especially when I'm alone. I have a job that I not only am good at and thrive in, but that I actively enjoy. Yet every day is blighted in some respect by various manifestations of bipolar disorder: anxiety, paranoia, intrusive thoughts, mood swings. By some standards, I'm absolutely not well. By others, I've "recovered."

I think this is what makes recovery such a slippery concept; there are no real parameters by which to judge it. Accepted knowledge recognizes this now, and recovery is seen as a journey or process rather than as a fixed point in time. This is how it should be—there's literally no way to measure wellness objectively, no way to quantify levels of mental illness with data, even if you do diligently fill in your mood diary every day.

But without the narrative of a journey or process, which I lacked, this vagueness made me feel disheartened with my progress. I wrongly believed that I'd one day be completely better, and that my life would resemble something that, in reality, it had never looked like to begin with. I thought "getting better" meant "everything will be perfect and nothing will go wrong ever again," and so every time something did go wrong, no matter how small, it felt like a crushing defeat. This belief is impractical on a number of levels, not least because small things go wrong all the time over the course of a life. Sometimes things fuck up at work. Sometimes someone dumps you. Sometimes you just wake up in a horrible mood for no reason whatsoever. I didn't take these as markers of a life lived fully, though—I saw them as dramatic missteps in my quest to get well.

To that end, I've pursued many things in the name of wellness: namely, medication and therapy.

MEDICATION 101

I have been on so many different medications that I genuinely no longer remember which I've taken and which I haven't. I was started on SSRIs—the classic, entry-level antidepressant. Fluoxetine and citalopram and paroxetine and sertraline: all impotent agents in the battle of my health. None of them worked for me—citalopram, for a while, made me less anxious, but on the whole they were pretty useless. This is not because they're useless generally, of course, but because for many years none of my doctors listened to what I was saying about my condition. I was just on the wrong medication.

Because I am bipolar, and SSRIs are largely prescribed for unipolar depression, in some cases they made things worse. Sertraline, commonly found in Zoloft, put me into a constant mixed state; I was incredibly agitated and antsy, had the drive of mania, but I was also despairing and angry and sad. The two feelings competed with each other, not quite canceling each other out. I would do a lot of the things I did when manic: talking endlessly at people, updating my Facebook status multiple times a day, and tweeting almost constantly. The only difference was that the joyful ebullience of mania was replaced with irritability and anger. I was tweeting all the time about how *angry* I was about things, about how *totally fucked up* I felt. It felt like shit. It was also really, really annoying for everyone else.

After my bipolar diagnosis, I was put on an antipsychotic, quetiapine. It made me so groggy I couldn't function, and it also made me balloon in weight; I went up two dress sizes in about a month, which didn't do much for my already shaky self-esteem. That was nothing compared to the other side effects, though; I was sleeping for twelve or thirteen hours a night, struggling to stay awake in the day. I'd sit on the bus on my way to work and often fall asleep, finding myself miles away from my office in some depot on the edge of the city, a bus driver telling me I had to get off. I'd fall asleep in meetings, and my already sparse social life slowed to a complete standstill. All I wanted to do was sleep, and sleep I did. I'd get in from work at six-thirty or seven at night and immediately get into bed, not waking up until the morning, when the whole horrible cycle would start again. Were I not employed, I have no doubt that I'd have spent twenty hours a day sleeping, and the other four in a horrible fugue state, stumbling around like a zombie.

I also discovered, to my horror, that taking my medication at the right time of day was actually imperative. I was used to winging it; it didn't really matter to me whether I took my contraception at 9:00 a.m. or 9:00 p.m., nor my antidepressants (though it's important to note that it's strongly encouraged that both of these kinds of drugs be taken at a regular time). I could not be so blasé about quetiapine. I forgot to take it one night when I came in from work—so, waking at 4:00 a.m., I decided to take my dose then. It was a mistake. I woke up when my alarm went off, unable to move. I wasn't coordinated at all; my legs literally didn't work. They crumbled underneath me as soon as I tried to stand up, and I couldn't speak. I tried to say something aloud to myself and a slurred jumble came out. I made my way to the toilet, which I could barely sit on, and back to bed. There was no way I was getting to work.

I decided to email my boss to tell him I had flu, as there was no way I could actually explain what had happened. I typed an email very slowly. Every letter was a tiny mountain, unconquerable by my jelly brain. Finally happy with my handiwork, I sent it and collapsed back into bed to sleep a dry-mouthed sleep. Later, I found, what I had sent was indecipherable nonsense, though at least my boss could tell I wasn't throwing a sickie for no reason (though he probably thought I was drunk or on drugs rather than dosed up on antipsychotics). Quetiapine had proved useful in the short term—my suicidal depression lifted fairly quickly, and my mood improved by quite some way—but the side effects were too much.

I wouldn't like to speculate about how normal my experience with medication is, and when I spoke to friends, I found a mixed bag. Some had gone on antidepressants and found that the medication had both lifted their mood and helped them stay stable; others had felt that it had exacerbated their problems or simply not helped. Some considered their medication a boring but vital part of their day-to-day lives; others saw it as a short-term solution to lift or change their moods during a particular episode, a tiny bandage to cover up temporary wounds.

The fact of the matter is, as with so many other things, it all comes down to personal experience, and asking questions and equipping yourself with knowledge about medication and all it entails can help.

What am I going to be prescribed?

The most commonly prescribed medications are antidepressants. SSRIs are likely to be the first port of call for most doctors, though which particular drug is chosen for you may be different for each doctor. There are a bunch of other antidepressants: SNRIs, tricyclics, MAOIs. For anxiety, there are also beta blockers and tranquilizers. For bipolar disorder, there are antipsychotics, anticonvulsants, and lithium. So the answer is, really: it depends what your diagnosis is and how your doctor feels it best to treat it.

How do I get medication?

There is one, and only one, answer to this: go to see a medical professional. Do not borrow drugs from your friend. Do not buy drugs on the internet. Do not self-medicate in any way. You need to see a doctor.

When I was finding it hard to sleep, I started taking Valium, which I'd bought off a friend who had obtained a bunch of the pills not exactly legally. I thought it was a great idea—I can't sleep, and Valium makes me sleep. What was the problem there?

The problem was that it hadn't been prescribed for me, and other than a brief browse through a few drug forums and Wikipedia, I didn't know much about it. It turns out it's incredibly addictive—so, in the long run, it made my sleeping worse.

When I ran out, and was unable to immediately obtain any more, I decided to go cold turkey. I felt awful, and my insomnia was even worse. I later went to see my psychiatrist, who prescribed me some proper sleeping pills, which I got through the much less risky portal of the local pharmacy. My psychiatrist knew my medical history; she had blood test results; she knew me and my experiences. It was much, much better than my own dodgy self-medicating, and much safer.

What will the side effects be?

The obvious answer here is that it depends what you're taking, but common side effects of antidepressants and antipsychotics can be nausea, dizziness, and loss of sex drive. One particularly egregious side effect of antidepressants, which seemed to affect me more than anything else, is tooth-grinding. When I was first put on citalopram, I spent about four days grinding my teeth and clenching my jaw, resulting in an incredibly sore mouth. It was like the day after taking a bunch of ecstasy, only I had had absolutely no fun throughout the entire experience.

With some meds, you may feel increased levels of depression or suicidal thoughts immediately after starting your course, which seems counterintuitive. Most of the time, this stops after a week or so, but if it doesn't, make another appointment with your doctor to see if you can find something that suits you better.

The best thing to do is ask your doctor about side effects, thoroughly read and take in the pamphlet that will come with your meds, and do your research online. Do not, however, take much notice of forum posts, which are often mildly terrifying.

Lots of people have bad experiences with medication, sure, but don't let that put you off—lots of people have good experiences too, they're just less likely to post about them online. This also goes for many of the side effects listed in the medication pamphlet. Yes, sudden death syndrome *might* occur for some people taking the same meds as you, but it is extremely, extremely unlikely, and you are far more likely to get a boring headache for three days instead.

The most recent medication I was prescribed—aripiprazole—can apparently cause "increased sexual interest" but also "swelling of the mouth, face, and tongue," which could have caused my love life to go one of two very distinct ways; in reality, I was fine on both counts.

Will it change my personality?

I think the thing I was most worried about before I went on medication was that I'd be somehow numbed to the world. I wouldn't be able to write, or I wouldn't feel things as deeply. This is a common worry. Whenever I talk to friends who are contemplating seeing their doctor about medication, it is one of their primary worries. But for all the various issues I've had with my medication, this has never been one of them.

Medication is not designed to numb you against the world, or to make you feel less. It's intended to rid you of depression or anxiety or mania, to make you more capable of coping. In fact, it doesn't make you *feel* anything in particular; it just makes you more stable. It evens you out. If anything, it makes it easier for you to actually be yourself again.

What happens if medication doesn't work?

First: *don't panic.* Medication often takes a while to settle in, and it may be a month or two before you see a real difference. One partner of mine told me that it had once taken eighteen months before his medication had settled down and started to make him feel better. You don't have to wait this long if you don't think your meds aren't working, but it's worth bearing in mind if you're feeling worried or impatient.

Plus, the first medication you try may not be for you, and that's fine. Try again. Go back to your doctor, and tell them it's not working out. If the pattern keeps repeating, rethink your options alongside your doctor, who may be able to further develop your treatment plan.

What will happen when/if I come off medications?

It's always best to come off your medication with the help or guidance of a doctor or therapist. I have learned from bitter, bitter experience that doing so is far preferable to going cold turkey. Cold turkey sucks. Cold turkey makes you feel physically and mentally terrible. Cold turkey is the worst.

If you do want to do it alone, make sure to taper your doses. Don't just stop taking it one day; start taking half doses, or taking them every other day until you slowly stop.

I don't recommend doing this without speaking to a doctor first, though. You're absolutely entitled to make up your own mind about this; even if they disagree, if you feel it's right for you to go med-free, then you do that thing. But the physical side effects of coming off medication can be just as severe or uncomfortable as the mental, so be careful.

There's a risk with medication and the way we talk about medication in wider culture: that it's seen as a complete antidote to whatever ailment you have. Documentaries and books about mental health stress that you *need* to be on medication. It's one of the first suggestions many doctors make, regardless of any underlying pressures or stresses you're experiencing at the time. To an extent, this is good—treating mental illness just as you would a physical illness can be demystifying, destigmatizing. You'd take antibiotics if you had an infection or a virus; why not treat mental health problems in exactly the same way?

But sometimes medication doesn't work. Sometimes it doesn't suit your lifestyle. Maybe you just don't want to be on medication. These are all fine, legitimate choices, and absolutely up to you.* I've been medication-free for several periods of my life. There's no need to feel pressured into doing what other people see as the "right thing" for you—if you're making a responsible, informed, and considered choice about medication, then it's your prerogative.

If you've never tried medication, however, my advice would be to try it out. There is always the chance—quite a strong chance, too—that medication *will* help. If it doesn't work, it doesn't work—it's a bummer, but it might happen. In the case of that happening, you're well within your rights to not want to be on anything, and

★ If you're still at an age where your parents can make medical decisions for you, rest assured that as soon as you come of age, you will be able to make such choices of your own volition.

to take charge of your mental health in a different way. But it's always worth finding that out for yourself.

THERAPY

Since I'm a complete narcissist, you would have thought I'd deeply enjoy therapy. After all, the literal point of therapy is that you sit and talk about yourself for an hour while a neutral party listens and asks questions about how you feel and what you think. It's the closest thing most of us are gonna get to being interviewed by Oprah, essentially. Yet, somehow, it's not quite as fun as that.

My main issue with therapy is that it genuinely forces me to examine how and why I do things. There's no self-deception involved here, just cold hard truths. Yes, your therapist is (or at least should be) neutral, but that doesn't mean they can't ask you incredibly awkward and searching questions. Less Oprah, more police interrogation.

I'm not being entirely serious, but this does get at why I have trouble going to therapy—because it genuinely *asks* something of you. Taking medication is a pretty amoral, value-free transaction—you put the pill in your mouth, you swallow, your mood is hopefully altered for the better. Therapy is harder than this. Therapy requires you to question your motives and work to adjust the imbalances in your behavior and your thoughts. Therapy requires you to be honest with yourself. Therapy requires you to take the time and effort to genuinely improve yourself as a person.

I *want* to go to therapy, because every time I've gone to therapy for a prolonged period of time, it's genuinely helped me. I *want* to be brave enough to look at my life and my choices and ask myself questions that need asking. And sometimes I am. Other times, I am not. If medication is a stiff drink after a bad day, therapy is a long hard look at yourself in the mirror the morning after.

There are lots of choices

There is an unimaginably huge range of choices for therapy and therapists. You may imagine yourself reclining on a couch while a Freudian psychoanalyst asks you about your childhood, and this may seem completely unappealing, but the range of options actually available is wider than that.

There's CBT, or cognitive behavioral therapy, which seeks to change the way you think and behave through the examination of thoughts, feelings, and behavior. There's psychoanalysis, which most closely resembles the Freudian stereotype. There's traditional talk therapy, where, rather predictably, you sit and talk through your issues. There are specific therapies for sexual dysfunction, anxiety, anger management, and more. There's hypnotherapy and art therapy, dialectic behavioral therapy. Essentially, there are a million types of therapies and therapists for a variety of different issues.

So do your research. What do you want to achieve during therapy? Do you want to resolve issues from your past, or do you want to focus on developing coping mechanisms for the future? What kind of therapist would make you feel most comfortable.

For example, do you want a male or female therapist? Do you have any specific requirements that might be worth considering—do you want a therapist specifically trained to deal with LGBT issues or someone who specializes in treating people who have experienced sexual assault or abuse? These things may not seem like they might affect your therapeutic journey much, but they really can; having someone you're completely comfortable with is the whole point, so you may as well be as specific as you possibly can be.

If you're still not sure, email or call a few different therapists to see whether or not they're the right fit for you.

My numerous bad experiences with therapy may seem off-putting, but perseverance really has been the key for me. Though I've had what feels like an endless list of pointless, boring, and sometimes potentially damaging therapy sessions, I'm now back in therapy and finding it—shock and horror—useful.

Making the effort to find a therapist I can relate to on a personal, psychological, and intellectual level has made all the difference for me—as with any ongoing relationship, it's important that you do genuinely relate to one another. Being liked isn't the point, obviously, but having an affable relationship with my therapist is very empowering. We're obviously not *friends,* because that's not the format of the relationship, but I can say that I feel liked, respected, and most of all *listened to.* It means I actually look forward to sessions I previously would have dreaded. It means I feel validated when I speak to him. (He also laughs at my bad jokes, which helps, though I suspect he does it out of politeness rather than genuine amusement.)

You will have to work hard

Somewhat annoyingly, therapy is hard work. You'll be forced to examine what you think and why you think it, and sometimes you'll have to examine your behavior. This can be revelatory, but often painful, and sometimes embarrassing or shameful.

You may also have to work through particularly difficult things—you may have experienced sexual assault, for example, and feel it's worth exploring with a therapist. You may have been putting off dealing with certain emotions or situations because it was the best way for you to cope at the time. This is fine, but therapy is often predicated on tackling these issues. It can be tough.

A good and responsible therapist will be sensitive to this, and will understand how hard—and sometimes awkward!—it will be for you to deal with and talk about these issues. That may not make it much easier for you to speak about your problems, but it can be reassuring to keep in mind when you're struggling to voice your feelings.

There are no easy answers, and there's certainly no cure

If you were expecting a transactional exchange—input hard emotional work, receive emotional revelation—you may be disappointed. While you may feel better for having therapy—I certainly have—it won't be instant, and it will never make you "not mentally ill." Some issues can absolutely be resolved, but others simply can't.

What it *can* do, though, is make you feel more stable and provide you with a steadier ground on which to build a more settled life. It can provide you with coping mechanisms that can actively prevent—or at least minimize—future episodes. I will always be bipolar, but I won't always seek comfort or distraction from bad episodes in the damaging ways I've relied on in the past, because therapy is teaching me how to at least attempt to deal with them in a healthier way. I've had moments of genuine, awe-inspiring revelation—*eureka* moments that have felt at first transcendentally important and then maddeningly obvious. Often, after these moments, I find myself asking myself why the fuck I hadn't previously been able to work out what now seemed like such a clear and self-evident truth. The answer is because *nobody had asked me the right question* and I didn't know how to direct myself toward it alone.

My current therapist combines CBT-type techniques with psychodynamic and humanistic approaches, which is working incredibly well for me. He asks me probing, interesting questions; he respects my boundaries; he constantly checks that I feel safe and able to carry on with sessions, especially when we're discussing difficult issues. Since I've started seeing him, I've consistently felt better equipped to deal with my problems, and have been far more self-critical in a way that's been incredibly constructive and productive. I feel like I'm constantly having lightbulb moments about my motivations and behaviors because I'm actually being encouraged to challenge them within the confines of an extremely safe space. In therapy, I can take responsibility for my mental health. I feel—for once—more stable.

RELAPSING

Relapsing is one of my worst fears. Give me shark-infested water or make me walk across the Grand Canyon on a tightrope any day, just, please god, don't let me relapse.

For those who don't know, relapsing essentially means moving away from a period of stability and contentedness to a period of ill mental health. This can happen at any point—you may have been feeling better again for a week or a year, and you may still experience a relapse.

Relapsing—which has happened to me often—is the number one reason I resolutely refuse to subscribe to the "it gets better" school of thought in mental illness. The thought *behind* "it gets better" is great—the point is that you won't feel like this forever. And that's true—you won't. At your very worst, you will get better. But that doesn't mean you'll be better forever, and that you won't feel that way again.

That said, there are plenty of things that can help or mitigate a relapse.

Watch out for triggers

Before you even experience a relapse, it's important to identify potential triggers. For me, breakups often lead to terrible depressive episodes, from drug binges to mania. Having to go out a lot, and thus losing sleep, can also make me manic, as can overexercising. Drinking too much can make me depressed; one particularly maudlin hangover can transport me from healthy and stable to fucked-up mess in no time at all. The list goes on.

It's taken me quite a long time to identify all of these triggers, and they're only the tip of the iceberg. There are many, many seemingly innocuous things that can trigger an episode for me. Be mindful of these. If you can, try to avoid them as much as possible. A good way to do this is to note them in your mood diary; see the back of the book for an example.

It's also important to note, however, that a relapse is often not triggered by anything. Sometimes there's absolutely nothing you did that causes you to feel bad again—it just happens. But it is useful to know what you need to keep an eye on.

Have a plan

This is advice that I've given throughout the book, but I can't stress it enough: have a wellness plan.

It's best to make both wellness plans and emergency plans with a professional, preferably your therapist. This can include a list of emergency contacts, a process for contacting people if you start feeling bad again, or a list of self-care ideas.

Make a list or a spreadsheet or fill a nice notebook full of pretty doodles and scrapbooked pictures—whatever works for you. Keep it somewhere safe, try to adhere to it as much as possible, and know exactly what to do when you need help. Share this with somebody else whom you trust. You essentially need to create an encyclopedia for yourself and your mental health.

Get help as soon as possible

If you feel yourself at the beginning of a relapse, **get help as soon as you can.** You may, like me, be prone to writing bad moods off as nothing more than a bad day, but it is vital that you keep an eye on yourself and your moods for wider patterns. One bad day is normal—a week or two weeks or a month of bad days is not. Struggling to get out of bed one morning or dreading work once a week is fine—feeling like that every day is not.

Once you start to see these patterns emerging—go and speak to someone. Mention it to a friend. Mention it to your therapist. Stopping depression or mania in their earlier stages isn't easy, but it's not impossible, and it is much, much less difficult than trying to squirm your way out of an incredibly bad episode.

Treat yourself kindly

And please, please remember: this is not the end of the world. It can be so, so disheartening when you've worked so hard at recovery and you feel like you're back at square one. It feels heartbreaking, actually; it feels like you did all that work for nothing, that you're going to feel this way forever, and that you're absolutely unfixable. **None of these things are true.**

The fact that you feel bad now doesn't undo all of the good work you've done before. If you've worked hard at recovery, then you'll know more about your mental illness than you can possibly imagine; you understand your moods better, you've gone to therapy, you've worked through issues, you've managed to maintain a stable and happy life for however long. These things aren't just suddenly invalidated because you're having a bad episode again. They've taught you things—things you might not be able to put into practice immediately, but things that will help you get better more quickly and efficiently. You know about SMART goals, so you can immediately put them into action; you know about self-care. Though it might feel like you're at square one, you're not. You've skipped back a few spaces, sure, but you're nowhere near the beginning.

My fear of relapsing may seem irrational to outsiders. Considering I've been ill for so long—*so* long—and have come out the other side of every major breakdown relatively unscathed, it should have lost some of its terrifying sheen by now. It hasn't.

Every moment of happiness is overshadowed by the threat of relapse. Every time I sit and plan for my future, I have to factor in a dreaded breakdown. When I think about where I want to be in ten years, of course I wonder and worry about my career and my relationships, whether I'll ever earn enough to buy a house, or whether I'll eventually get my driving license. But in amongst all of that stuff—the regular twentysomething stuff—I think *What happens to my career if I have to take time off to recover from a suicide attempt?* and *Will my relationships survive if I have a particularly bad manic episode?* Will I even be alive, more to the point? Will I be able to keep surviving episode after episode of bad mental health?

My multiple trips to psychiatric hospitals and doctors' surgeries and the horrible, drug-addled lows of my life should probably have served as lessons. Y'know—things can only get better! When you hit rock bottom, the only way is up! That kind of thing. All of these things should serve as vaccination against fear; I should be immune. I know what to do, after all. I know the score.

But when you've "recovered," when you've slowly built your life up again, the idea that it could all disappear is even more terrifying. I have a pretty nice life now; I have a tiny cat and an apartment I like living in. I get to write about things that I care about, and people actually pay me money for it. I hate to say it, but I genuinely like my life. What if it's taken away again?

But you know what? That's not how I should look at it. My apartment and my cat, this book and my friends and my job are not things that *can* be taken away from me. In a literal sense, obviously, I could lose my job or fall out with my friends, or accidentally poison my cat. Every copy of this book could be destroyed in a simultaneous pulp plant/hard drive deletion accident. But in a metaphorical sense—because yes, we're getting deep here—they're immovable.

What they represent is a talent that I have, and that everyone mentally ill has, for rebuilding. It might not be a talent that we want—I feel like I'd rather *not* know how rock bottom feels, or how exactly you proceed from that point. But we have it out of necessity. Everything you have—whether that's a lot or a little—is testament to your continued existence, and the strength that that necessitates.

Sometimes recovery feels genuinely impossible, and once you're there, it feels tentative and unsteady and altogether ready to completely collapse. We all know that it's a distinct possibility—unless you're one of the incredibly lucky people who experience only one period of bad mental health in their lives, you're likely to feel like shit again at some point.

But if and when you do relapse, go forward with the knowledge that you *can* rebuild things, you *can* cope. You know how to look after yourself when you're feeling like shit. You know what to tell a doctor. You know how to tell your mum or your girlfriend or your teachers how you feel and what help you need. You understand yourself better as a result of this. You may even have learned things about yourself that you'd previously underestimated. Being mentally ill isn't fun or enjoyable by any stretch of the imagination, but it can give you this deeper well of understanding, a way of navigating the world slightly differently. After a while, you'll know how better to help yourself, and you'll be able to do it more efficiently, more eloquently, more sensitively. You might even like yourself more (or at least a bit).

In other words? You got this.

RESOURCES

FURTHER SUPPORT

National Suicide Prevention Lifeline

http://www.suicidepreventionlifeline.org/

1-800-273-8255

The National Hopeline Network

1-800-SUICIDE (1-800-784-2433)

1-800-SUICIDA (1-800-784-2432) (Spanish-Speaking)

Crisis Textline

http://www.crisistextline.org/

Text START to 741-741

The National Grad Crisis Line

Free, confidential telephone counseling for graduate students, crisis intervention, suicide prevention, and information and referral services

1-877-GRAD-HLP (877-472-3457)

I'm Alive

Online chat network

https://www.imalive.org/

The Trevor Project

Focuses specifically on suicide prevention in LGBTQ youth

http://www.thetrevorproject.org/

1-866-488-7386

Note: They also have a text and online chat service on their website.

Trans Lifeline

http://www.translifeline.org/

1-877-565-8860

International Foundation for Research and Education on Depression

www.ifred.org

Substance Abuse and Mental Health Services Administration

http://www.samhsa.gov/

1-800-662-HELP (1-800-662-4357)

National Alliance on Mental Illness

http://www.nami.org/

1-800-950-NAMI (1-800-950-6264)

Depression and Bipolar Support Alliance (DBSA)

www.dbsalliance.org

American Psychiatric Association

www.psychiatry.org

1-703-907-7300

Anxiety and Depression Association of America

www.adaa.org

1-240-485-1001

Note: This phone number is not a crisis line, and you will likely be prompted to leave a voice mail.

MentalHealth.org

http://www.mentalhealth.org/

National Institute of Mental Health

http://www.nimh.nih.gov/index.shtml

1-866-615-6464

S.A.F.E. Alternatives

http://www.selfinjury.com/

1-800-DONTCUT (1-800-366-8288)

Mental Health Works (Canada)

http://www.mentalhealthworks.ca/

1-877-977-5580

Mood Disorders Society of Canada

https://mdsc.ca/

1-519-824-5565

Self Injury Outreach and Support (Canada)

http://sioutreach.org/

MOOD DIARIES

Mood diaries can be incredibly useful both for you and for your clinician or therapist. There are online resources that allow you to keep a mood diary, as well as several apps, and you can create a mood diary via a Google Docs spreadsheet. You can also keep an old-fashioned mood diary on paper; an example is on the next page.

DAY, TIME, AND LOCATION	MOOD/EMOTION	COMMENTS *(who were you with, what were you doing, what went through your mind, what triggered it)*
Wednesday 11 a.m., at school	Unhappy—3/10	Told off at school. Felt humiliated in front of classmates.
Thursday 9 p.m., at home	Lonely—4/10	On my own, spending time on the internet, wished I was seeing friends.
Friday 7 a.m., on the bus	Anxious—3/10	Triggered by lack of sleep.

BREATHING AND RELAXATION EXERCISES

There are so many different breathing exercises you can try that there's no way I could possibly include all of them. But below are a few examples that have helped me in the past.

The basics

Lie or sit somewhere comfortably. If you're sitting, cross your legs and keep your back straight and shoulders back.

Close your eyes.

Breathe in deeply through your nose for five seconds, or to the count of five (as long as this is comfortable for you), feeling the breath flow from as far down your body as you can.

Hold your breath for two seconds.

Breathe out, again counting to five, through your mouth.

Do this for several minutes, or for as long as you need to feel calmer.

"Belly breathing"

Lying down, place one hand on your stomach and the other on your chest.

Gently breathe out, letting your upper body relax as you do it.

Pause for a few seconds.

Inhale through your nose for a few seconds and pause again. Repeat, focusing on relaxing your muscles.

Progressive Muscle Relaxation

This is the exercise I find most helpful. It completely calms me down, and I often use it to help me go to sleep. You can do this sitting in a chair or lying down, although if you lie down, you may also fall asleep.

The first step is actually making your body *more* tense. Methodically work your way up your body, from your feet, tensing your muscles as you go. Squeeze your feet up as hard as you can…and relax. Squeeze your leg muscles as hard as you can…and relax. Move all the way up your body, tensing and relaxing every part of your body for five or ten seconds.

SMART GOAL TABLE

SPECIFIC—What is the goal? Break it down into several small steps.
MEASURABLE—How are you going to measure it? Are you aiming to cut down on something or quit completely? Put a figure on it.
ACHIEVABLE—Write down the steps you need to take to make this happen.
RELEVANT—What resources do you need to achieve this? How are you going to do it? Write this down.
TIMELY—When do you want to do it by? 1:00 p.m.? Tomorrow morning? The end of the year?

INDEX

ACKNOWLEDGMENTS

First off, I have to thank my wonderful, patient, tenacious, brilliant agent Robyn Drury, who was not only the catalyst for me writing this book but has also dealt with numerous mini-breakdowns and thousands of emails over the last eighteen months with patience and good humor and never once replied to a stupid question of mine with "can't you just Google it?!" as she probably could have and should have done. I'd also like to thank everyone else at Diane Banks for being so supportive throughout the whole process, despite the fact I had absolutely no idea what I was doing at any given moment.

I'd also like to thank everyone at Sourcebooks for helping me with this project—especially my editor, Grace Menary-Winefield, who has been the most encouraging, positive cheerleader throughout the process (even when I've been dangerously cavalier with my deadlines). I couldn't have done it without you.

To everyone who agreed to be interviewed for the book: Felicity de Vere, for her medical know-how; Billy MacFarlane, for talking to me about teaching; Jonny Gabriel, for talking to me about his brother, Simon; and everyone else who anonymously shared anecdotes, stories, and experiences with me while I wrote the book.

I also want to say thank you to all of my friends, who have put up with me saying variants upon "I am writing a book, and I am stressed about writing the book" for nearly two straight years. (Sorry about that.)

Firstly, everyone (and there are way too many to mention by name) from the creepy dog crew/alt Twitter, for distracting me all day and inviting me to brunch every weekend when I definitely should have been writing this book. All my Berlin friends, who had to listen to me talk about nothing but edits for about six weeks. For proofreading, suggestions, thought-provoking debates, general encouragement, and pep talks, I'd also like to say thanks to George Berridge, Tristan Cross, Josh Hall, Merlin Jobst, Sarah-Louise Kelly, Tom Mendelsohn, Alison Terpstra, Jack Urwin, and James Vincent. This is the only time I'm ever going to be sincere to any of you (and in actual print, *ugh*), but I love you all and am deeply appreciative of all the help and support you've given me re: the book and also re: my being crazy. Special thanks to George Allen and Tilly Steele, the two people I could never live without—two brilliant, sparkling, fascinating, and talented people who have made me a way better person simply by allowing me to be myself.

To my therapist, Anthony Rhone, who somehow managed to help me start to craft a vaguely humanlike form out of what was previously a weird, amorphous, dysfunctional blob.

To all of my family I want to say thanks but also sorry—thank you for putting up with me, looking after me, and bailing me out of every stupid mess I've ever made; sorry that you had to.

Most of all, I'd like to thank anybody who has ever got in touch with me to talk about mental health: people's sisters and wives and boyfriends and best friends who wanted to know how to help; people who wanted to tell me their stories or ask me for advice or just talk to someone else who gets it; people who are desperately ill and people who are in recovery. This book is about you and for you, and I hope that by telling my story, I've done justice to yours.

ABOUT THE AUTHOR

Photo credit © Jamie Drew 2017

Emily Reynolds is a writer/broadcaster from London. She specializes in mental health, technology, science, and feminism, writing for *Buzzfeed*, *VICE*, and *Wired*, among many others. She was diagnosed with bipolar disorder in her early twenties, and since then has been raising awareness and supporting other young people with mental health issues. She also cofounded the Words by Women Awards in 2016.

Made in the USA
Monee, IL
21 July 2025

21611905R00154